THE REAL COST

OF FAKE NEWS

5. 17. 19

A Collector's Edition
- I hope you don't mind
there are a few spelling
errors that have since
been fixed.
Happy to get you a fresh
copy.   Savita

THE REAL COST OF FAKE NEWS

THE HIDDEN TRUTH BEHIND THE PLANNED PARENTHOOD VIDEO SCANDAL

DR. SAVITA GINDE

Printed in the United States of America.
Library of Congress Control Number: 2018955226
ISBN Paperback: 978-0-578-40431-8
ISBN eBook: 978-1-949639-02-5

Cover Design: Kerry Ellis

He gives not the best who gives the most

But he gives the most who gives his best.

If I cannot give bountifully yet I will give freely,

And what I lack in my hand I will supply with my heart.

ANONYMOUS

TABLE OF CONTENTS

PROLOGUE

ON AUGUST 3, 2015, I fled my home in the dark of night, flanked by armed security, with my then thirteen-month-old twins, husband, and our family pet. I can't believe those words are a part of my life's journey. I had to flee my home. The home that I so lovingly planned, for which I'd picked out wood floors and light fixtures, and had even gone to the quarry warehouse where I picked out the granite slab that was to become the countertop in my kitchen. The countertop on which cakes were mixed, brunches served, and family dinners created.

I had to flee my home. My eyes still well with tears, a lump forms in my throat, and I feel a knot in my stomach every single time those words go through my head. That reality, even years later, still seems surreal. I don't believe that the behavior that forced us to flee our home is laudable, honorable, or even acceptable. How does this happen in the United States of America? What's happened to this country? I thought we were better than this.

My husband and I knew that we owed an explanation to our many friends and acquaintances across our small neighborhood. We loved our neighborhood, and we personally knew many of our neighbors. So, soon after fleeing our home, we sent the following e-mail to all of them:

From: Savita Ginde
Date: August 16, 2015 at 9:13:19 PM MDT
Subject: From Your Concerned Neighbor

Dear Neighbors,

I wanted to offer a little context [for] current circumstances because it might impact you, or you might have questions about recent events around our neighborhood.

I live in Deer Valley and I work for Planned Parenthood of the Rocky Mountains. Planned Parenthood is the most trusted women's health care provider in this country. We have provided birth control, life-saving cancer screenings, pregnancy options information (including adoption, parenting, and legal termination services), and other high-quality health care for 99 years. Less than 3% of what Planned Parenthood does involves pregnancy termination services. One in five American women reports having been to Planned Parenthood for care. I'm proud to be a medical provider for Planned Parenthood of the Rocky Mountains, because we have the highest professional standards and we care deeply for our patients.

Recently, an extremist anti-Planned Parenthood group has released several videos that have been shown to be heavily edited in order to completely distort what people on the tapes are actually saying. These videos are a fraud, intended to shock and deceive the public. For example, one video was edited to make it look like a doctor said she would "sell" fetal tissue for a profit—when in fact she said the exact opposite 10 separate times, and nearly all instances were edited out of the tape. I was secretly recorded and shown in one of these deceptive videos. They pasted together the conversation and even attributed phrases and statements to me that I did not say. This was done to demonize me and my work. I do not engage in fetal tissue donation or any program involving fetal tissue, and never have, ever. The outrageous claims being made about Planned Parenthood and about my work are completely false. The extremists who released these heavily edited videos are engaged in a fraud, and other claims they've made have been discredited and disproven. These extremists are known liars and will stop at nothing to try to prevent women from safe and effective birth control options and reproductive health care.

I want you to be aware that our privacy is currently being invaded, our lives threatened, and we remain the target of bullying and harassment by these extremists. This is what these extremists hope to accomplish—to bully, harass, invade, threaten, and attempt to intimidate. Unbelievably, they do all this while referencing the Lord Jesus Christ; this is blasphemy of all that He stood for and all that He is.

We believe these extremists are false prophets.

They have personally distributed and even mailed flyers across our beautiful, quiet neighborhood—flyers with material of false content for shock value and intended to disparage women's health providers like me. I apologize in advance for any inconvenience or anxiety this may cause you.

These tactics have caused safety concerns for me and my family and might impact you, my neighbors. We are sorry if the picketers and the people trespassing across our entire community create problems for you or your family. We ask that you report anything or anyone suspicious to Police (non-emergent line) as soon as possible. Of course, you can also call 911 if necessary.

We love our home and our neighborhood, and just like you, we want to live a life of freedom, tolerance, and happiness. Like you, we do not believe that attempting to frighten and harass people is acceptable, anywhere and for any reason. We strive to keep Deer Valley a safe and peaceful neighborhood.

Sincerely,
Savita & her family

*

I am a doctor, and this is my story. Though my profession is that of a physician, and my job, at the time, was serving as the chief medical officer for Planned Parenthood of the Rocky Mountains, my job is just one facet of who I am.

I write this as the wife of a loving and supportive husband, the mother of twins, the daughter of wise and caring parents, a sister, a friend, a colleague, a neighbor, and so much more—including a woman of faith and spirituality. As I give you a glimpse into the impact of these fictional videos, I am writing this as a multifaceted human because the videos have impacted all areas of my life.

I thought life became a juggling act when my twins were born, but nothing has compared to our journey over the last couple of years. I actually finished this book over a year ago but, as I got closer to my initial launch date, I left Planned Parenthood and, I must admit, it cleared my head and gave my family and me time to heal and connect with people who truly wished for our health and well-being. My departure from Planned Parenthood of the Rocky Mountains was handled with nothing but unprofessional, vindictive, and disgraceful behavior by the ever-indignant CEO, Vicki Cowart. It's a shame. She had a choice, and yet elected to display nothing but negativity. She's always battling to remain in control, never caring to do the right thing. But she is just one lost person; she is not Planned Parenthood. Nevertheless, I am committed to sharing my story and my perspective; I find more often than not, media fails at connecting the dots that would resolve division and put us, as a country, on a path toward unification. Here goes . . .

In July of 2015, following a multiyear infiltration led by a well-known anti-abortion extremist named David Daleiden, a series of deceptively edited videos were released attempting to implicate Planned Parenthood in the selling of fetal tissue. These allegations are not only completely false, but in the videos in which I am featured many of my words are taken out of context, other words are actually dubbed in, and actions are attributed to me that never actually happened. The words and actions are completely false—literally, FAKE NEWS—and nevertheless, the immediate aftermath of the infiltration was devastating.

My family's once-peaceful life was turned upside down within a matter of minutes. As my husband has said on a number of occasions since the edited and false videos were released, "If you have to lie to make a point, you don't really have a point."

The false videos led to a national—actually, an *international*—campaign of hate for me as an individual; one that was so intense that I had 24/7 armed security assigned to me after the release of the second video on July 30, 2015. To give you an exact flavor of this intensity, I am going to share just two of the many e-mail messages, voicemail messages, and social media posts that I received after the videos were released:

> *I see that you are a fucking monster who sells crushed babies. I would like to recommend you as evil fucking person, cautious baby cruncher, baby parts merchant,*

baby parts separator, cannibal, baby sell out, and top 100 evil persons of 2015.

That was sent directly to me on my LinkedIn account from a total stranger.

And here's another:

One thing I am ashamed of is that this is Savita, my sister in law. [...] She and those like her belong in jail. I love my brother, but I could not condone his wife's actions and his support of them any more than if he had married into the KKK, Nazi party, or ISIS. [...] I am not willing to give up my deepest held moral basis in the fundamental value of human lives. If the price I pay is the estrangement from my own flesh and blood, then so be it.

In case that wasn't clear, that is an excerpt of a post my husband's brother wrote on a family Facebook page, which also included a direct link to the deceptive and fake videos.

So, how did we get here? Why the fake news?

In this book, I will set the record straight and share my side of the story, with the truth and the facts. But this book is also about tolerance and finding a path forward. My story is but one story. In the more than two years since this happened, I have seen the essence of what launched this specific fake-news campaign rear its ugly head again and again: division, an "us and them" mentality, and a comfort in limiting our interactions with those we believe to be like-minded—a conscious bias.

This is short-sighted. Let's rekindle our love of diversity and reignite our curiosity in our differences. Really, we cannot and should not all be the same, right? How boring, how stifling, how narrow. Is there a gain or, maybe, a security in forcing everyone to fall into one single line?

I really hope to change the conversation about a person's right to decide the best path forward for his or her life and family. When I say this, I am talking about moving this so-called "war" into a conversation, one with civil objectives, rules of engagement, and constructive, realistic solutions. I want to talk about a path forward for everyone in this country who has a right to believe what he or she believes—but doesn't have a right to terrorize, intimidate, or violate another person's world. Some of this is law and much of this comes from a place of basic human civility and decency. Let's raise the bar.

CHAPTER 1

THE BEGINNING

I WAS BORN in Toledo, Ohio, and grew up in a city called Youngstown. Even though I'm American, I grew up in a family that legally immigrated here as the United States was looking for physicians to work in underserved areas of various states across our great country. My parents were born in India, and my sister in the UK; I was born in America.

My parents raised us to be very independent and strong. They have always been very supportive of my taking every opportunity that I could; they wanted both my sister and me to really reach our potential.

Throughout my life, we traveled a lot. We used to go to India every summer when my grandparents were alive. This took place throughout my mid-teens, before they passed away.

When we would visit, our Indian family would sometimes poke fun at us because we were so *American* in their eyes. They would say, "We can tell you're not from here, even though you wear Indian clothes. We can tell by the way you walk and how you talk." Or they would say, "Even

1

though you speak the language, you don't sound like us. You sound like Americans trying to speak the language." We'd thought our accents were spot on.

I come from a family of doctors and if the topic of reproductive health ever came up, Indian family members would say things like, "Oh, you American people. You have way too much time on your hands to get into other people's personal business."

From their perspective, they said they were more worried about their own day-to-day lives and making everything work. You know, getting food on the table and making ends meet. They said they didn't have time to worry about what the neighbor was doing—if she was on birth control or whatever.

What a contrast this is when compared to the state of reproductive justice in America! I also knew there was this big issue of religion, including some faiths that I didn't really know much about or that I didn't understand. Growing up, we went to an all-girls private Catholic high school. That's where I got my real introduction to Catholicism. The school was run by nuns, and yet we were raised Hindu. I embraced this opportunity to learn more about and experience Catholicism. I mean, why not? I was astonished to know so many devout Catholics who used birth control in spite of the official view of the Church, which declared that it was forbidden. Whenever I inquired about this to gain a better understanding, the same response was always given: "I have to do what is best/right for me and my family," and other statements on how real life was more important in their decision-making than the impossible goals of appearing to be perfect. That was my first glimpse into a group of people who pretended to subscribe to the tenets of their religion and then turned around and acted in a way that they felt they needed to act; but who are they lying to? My understanding is that God is omniscient, so they aren't getting away with anything there.

I engage my personal faith as a path to "doing the right thing." I was raised with the notion that the growth of my being was based on my personal relationship with my god. My mom would boil it down like this: "You look at yourself in the mirror at night and you have to be OK with all that you've done. And if you're not OK with something, then you need to reconcile what you've done so you will not make that mistake again. This is how you become a better person. It shouldn't ever really matter what anyone else says or thinks. You can listen to everyone's guidance but—always know— they, too, are on the same path."

If we did something wrong, I still remember my dad's words to me as a teenager: "There are three ways to deal with things. You can watch other people make mistakes and learn from that. You can make the mistakes yourself and learn from them. Or you can be totally unaware of what you're doing and keep making the same mistakes again and again. The choice is yours."

Needless to say, I have made a lot of mistakes. I've tried to use every single one as an opportunity to reflect, learn, grow, and move forward. After an appropriate period of reflection, I always visualize myself getting up off of the ground, brushing myself off, and carrying on. I aim for no regrets while I also accept my humanity. Though I graduated from the University of Pennsylvania, I hadn't set myself up for success. I was waitlisted at medical schools and eventually made the choice to start my first two years at a medical school in the British West Indies. I thought it would be fine. I thought that when I came back, I would just fit right in and stay on track. I was wrong.

Growing up, I knew I was capable and smart. Not necessarily "the" smartest, but I could excel with some effort. However, when I came back from the British West Indies, I had people treating me poorly for the first time in my life. I was looked down upon for not going to medical school in the States.

At first I was horrified, and I struggled to deal with this. But then I embraced it. I took it as a challenge to prove just how capable I really was, and it actually changed my life. This was important for me because it made me realize that I had been privileged my entire life. I have been given every opportunity and had never heard someone say, "We can't afford to do this," or "You can't go there," or "You can't do this."

But when I found myself struggling, I knew it wasn't because of my abilities or any lack thereof. It was because of my circumstances. I was disadvantaged because of circumstance. Granted, this was a situation that I had chosen, but the level of discrimination was something I had never imagined. My heart ached as I realized that others around me, my fellow humans, could be in that same situation—disadvantaged by circumstance—and have no way out. This experience, the realization, definitely drove my next steps, and likely steered me to Planned Parenthood, which is where I worked during the fake-video release and "baby parts" scandal of 2015.

I eventually connected my professional work with my passion for wanting to help people, regardless of their background, experiences, education, or circumstance. I was going to contribute in whatever small way I could to help people who didn't have the same opportunities or access to resources that I did growing up.

*

As I finished my residency in Family Medicine, I started to develop an interest in gynecology and women's health. Never once did it cross my mind that because of my medical interest that my life was ever going to be in danger. In 2001, I began a two-year fellowship in family planning in upstate New York at the University of Rochester. The fellowship involved our going to the local Planned Parenthood.

One of the lessons our program director planned for us was to go talk to some of the protesters outside of that Planned Parenthood. He told us to ask questions and to try to have a conversation with those protestors. More than anything, he told us to listen. I distinctly remember trying to have a conversation with one man who was a regular protestor. I remember asking a very basic question: "Why are you out here?" But he simply repeated the same Bible verse back to me again and again, his voice rising with each repetition. We couldn't even have a conversation. What he was saying to me, repeatedly, didn't even make sense. I remember asking myself, *If we can't even have a conversation, how do we change this? How can we find a middle ground?* It was another pivotal moment for me.

We were at this Planned Parenthood regularly during my fellowship, but this was the only time we went across the road to talk to the protesters. By then I had learned about Dr. Barnett Slepian—an obstetrician who provided abortions in Buffalo—who was shot through his kitchen window by an anti-choice person in the fall of 1998. He was the third abortion doctor murdered in the US since 1993.

According to a *New York Times* article about the event, Dr. Slepian and his family had dealt with years of picketing and harassment. As a result, they'd moved to a quieter neighborhood a couple years earlier to get away from the protestors.[1]

I couldn't get that story out of my head. I also kept thinking about the conversation I'd tried to have with that protestor outside Planned Parenthood. I quickly discovered that many of the people standing outside clinics protesting were not only incapable of engaging in civil discourse, they also weren't safe to be around. This was the first time I started

---

1   Jim Yardley and David Rohde, "Abortion Doctor in Buffalo Slain; Sniper Attack Fits Violent Pattern," *New York Times*, October 25, 1998.

to think of that group of people as domestic terrorists: people who don't care to or just can't have a civil conversation or respectful debate about different beliefs, faiths, or morals *and* who will behave violently or incite violence because one does not agree with their belief, faith, or morals. Ironically, this is very similar to how ISIS operates, and these similarities are downright disturbing.

Knowing what I know now, I can't believe I went over there to try to speak with the protestors. But I was young. It was my first year of fellowship and I was just starting out. I am still, to this day, trying to understand why protestors stand on their religion to bully, harass, and—even worse— promote violence and murder, and yet they can't even have a conversation about the beliefs that drive them, and they refuse to accept anyone who doesn't believe exactly the way that they do.

But my work at Planned Parenthood during my fellowship was meaningful and I enjoyed my time there. I noticed right away that the providers were caring and skilled, and most importantly, I recognized that they respected their patients. Everyone was well informed. I still stand by that today. I watched providers give as much information as possible to their patients. They talked to them about *all* of their options. I know that some people think (incredibly) that Planned Parenthood only provides abortions, but I see it another way: Planned Parenthood provides choices—information, education, and realistic paths, so that men and women can make well-informed decisions about what is right for them.

I finished my fellowship and was ready to launch my career. I was looking for a position where I could incorporate all of the things I enjoyed from the fellowship program. I wanted to take care of patients, specifically within the reproductive-health and family-planning field. So that included abortion care and contraception, as well as clinical training and clinical research. I had built a solid foundation of clinical research experience as a fellow and was interested in continuing to contribute to new technologies and innovation. I also loved training medical students and residents. I wanted to do all of these things, and I started to wonder if Planned Parenthood would be a good fit.

CHAPTER 2

COLORADO

WHEN I FINISHED my fellowship, I was open to moving wherever I wanted. I was ready for something new and, after visiting a friend in Colorado, I fell in love with the place. I set out to find a job, and I found one at Planned Parenthood of the Rocky Mountains (PPRM). PPRM had an open position for something like director of surgical services. I applied when I got home from my Colorado trip, and, soon enough, the medical director offered me the job. I finished my fellowship, took a month off, and then moved myself out to Colorado toward the end of 2003. In the month leading up to my move, I e-mailed the PPRM medical director to say that I was all done with my training and I asked where and when I should show up. I didn't receive a reply. I began to grow nervous as I packed my boxes and took care of last-minute arrangements. I didn't hear a peep. It turns out that the medical director who had hired me had suffered a heart attack and died. It took the administrators a little while to go through his e-mail messages and eventually get back to me.

They were still scrambling to pick up the pieces and get

things in order when I showed up, so they put me in their call center where I helped them answer clinical questions. A couple months later, they told me that they were opening up the position for medical director and asked if I wanted to apply. I did, and I got the job.

It was a pretty amazing job because I got to do all the things I enjoyed in medicine. I was actively involved at the leadership table, and over the course of my time there I developed a highly respected family-planning training program and a solid clinical research division, and I engaged a cadre of qualified physicians and advanced practice providers to work for the organization. Everyone was committed to making sure patients received the high-quality clinical care they deserved, coupled with accurate, evidence-based information.

I also learned how to simultaneously manage multiple clinics at a distance and across multiple states—in Colorado, Wyoming, Nevada, and New Mexico. When I first joined PPRM, I even provided medical oversight to a clinic in West Virginia and two in Missouri. Nevertheless, I spent most of my time working in the metro-Denver area. I also frequently worked in Ft. Collins or in Colorado Springs. I knew the staff well at both clinics, and some felt like family to me.

My concerns over security at Planned Parenthood started pretty much right away. Our administrative offices used to be in a completely separate location from where we would do our clinical work, so I would have to travel to the surgical site to do my patient care. One of the surgical sites was about five miles away from the administrative office. There were a bunch of really loud, nasty protestors around that building and it was just poorly set up. We had to always drive through the protestors to get into work—and believe me, they didn't make it easy. There was always this fear that you might accidentally hit one of them. As much as they harassed us, obviously, we didn't want to hurt anyone. They were always in our faces and standing all around the car as we pulled in. Sometimes they would have these big cameras shoved in our faces as we got out and tried to walk into work.

One time they threw nails on the ground and I ended up getting a flat tire on my way home. The building wasn't strategically designed to protect the staff, the physicians, or the patients when coming in and out of the building. There was a definite feeling of vulnerability. Even at the time, I didn't understand why the protestors were allowed to be in such close proximity to us or why harassing people was in any way worthwhile. I know about the laws and freedoms of this country, but behavior such as this doesn't respect anyone and there is no dignity in their actions. Why do we allow people to do that? Why don't we push back in some way and say you can't get up close to the cars, you can't bully, and you sure as hell can't say that your behavior is sanctioned by your religion?

I started asking questions about security almost immediately. I was really interested in proactively protecting everyone's privacy.

This way of life didn't necessarily become normal—

because it was never comfortable—but it did become expected. I expected that when I got to work, I was going to have a couple moments of terror and I was just going to have to learn how to manage that terror. And then I would extend those resources and terror-management skills to the other physicians who worked for us so that they would feel supported and proactively engaged in protecting themselves and their families.

My main coping mechanism was preparedness. I left the rest to the universe. If I didn't want to have my picture taken, I would have a certain way of getting out of my car with my back turned. Or sometimes I would wear sunglasses and a hat. Internally, the staff and providers really had to learn to be there for each other. I don't think there's any other field where you have this kind of experience.

During those first few years, Facebook was starting to make its presence known and other social media platforms were growing as well. The protestors outside Planned Parenthood followed suit. Before, when a protester would take a photo, you would question what they were going to do with the picture. But now, with social media taking over people's lives, we knew we were going to be immortalized on the Internet. Many of us are.

Suddenly there were things all over the Web. Websites with a map of the USA, where you could click on any state and physicians who provide abortions would be listed by state, with their pictures and home addresses. There would be calls to action, to descend on people's homes and neighborhoods, a constant and continued rallying of the masses to bully and harass the providers. As social media became a bigger part of everyone's lives, we really had to think more strategically. How much of our lives were we willing to give up?

Within a few years of that initial setup where we had separate administrative and patient-care facilities, we built a new site where Planned Parenthood of the Rocky Mountains remains today. Now the administrative building and the clinic are combined in one building. It's simpler and everything is in one place. When we were building that clinic, the protestors went so far as to show up at the construction folks' houses to try and harass and intimidate them and their families. This is one of their common tactics. They find out who's working with us in any capacity, and then go out there and try to wear them down. For instance, they did this with Stericycle. The anti-choice leadership will ask business staff, "Why are you supporting these people?" They have even done this with the United States Postal Service, UPS, and FedEx.

All this does is contribute to the divisiveness of the US. It forces companies to start injecting their personal religious beliefs into their business. The truth is, sometimes the workers and businesses would fold on Planned Parenthood. And I get it; it's a lot to ask somebody to withstand that kind of pressure.

As a doctor, we were there every day trying to help people. For most physicians who work in family planning, it has got to be a calling or a passion to put yourself in that sort of a position—versus having a practice that isn't associated with family planning or Planned Parenthood.

But for a general contractor who is building a site, if protestors are harassing him, I'm sure that the incentive to withstand it is probably a lot lower than it is for my physicians or me. We've had some contractors say, "This is a job just like any other job. We're not taking sides," which I think is a great way to look at things. But when protesters are at your house, threatening your family, and invading not only your space, but also all of your neighbors' spaces, it becomes a big deal—a really big deal. Unfortunately, domestic terrorism sometimes works.

In those first few years at Planned Parenthood, we were used to protestors being there. It was a part of our daily lives. They would shout at anyone who was coming or going, whether that person was a staff member, a physician, a patient, or a companion. But it wasn't until about 2011— about seven years into my time there—that they started calling me out by name. By that point, I was married, and so I had another person deeply invested in my safety.

My husband works in security and information technology, and he occasionally does training with law enforcement. Right off the bat, he noted that the security we were offered at Planned Parenthood was inadequate. But what could we do?

*

I met my husband in 2007 and we were married a little

over a year later.

By then, social media was ramping up even more. It became apparent pretty quickly that while Planned Parenthood acknowledged that the protesters existed, they didn't have tools in place to proactively provide security for their physicians. It didn't even feel like they acknowledged that we were specific targets, despite the provider assassinations that had already occurred.

So, my husband and I put our heads together and came up with some tools to make things feel a little safer for me. We took it upon ourselves to lock everything down with our social media accounts and we unknowingly started to build a little bit of a program.

First, we trained ourselves on the best practices for social media and online safety. We adjusted privacy settings and set up Google alerts. Google alerts can be extremely helpful for continuous monitoring of the Internet. Setting up a Google alert with your name will enable you to receive e-mail notifications when new results show up in a Google search with mentions of your name. Of course, this is easier with a unique first and last name like mine, but it is nonetheless a useful, no-cost step for anyone who wants to be proactive about personal safety.

We didn't even have kids yet but we set up as much privacy and restriction that would allow us to communicate with friends and family without compromising our security. This felt important to us. Once we worked through some best practices, we extended that training to the rest of my providers and openly shared our knowledge and strategies with colleagues across the country whenever asked.

Eventually, my husband and I knew we must be doing something right, as Planned Parenthood's national office, PPFA, started sending people our way. They would have new hires, such as a new medical director or a new provider, call them, asking what to do or how to best protect themselves. And PPFA would basically say, "Call Ginde. She and her husband will tell you." We used to spend hours with these people on the phone, telling them everything they could do—from setting up Google Alerts to beefing up their social media security settings, to becoming aware of their vulnerabilities on the Internet and understanding the tactics anti-choice people use, such as following you home to learn your address. Becoming conscious of our Internet presence and day-to-day vulnerabilities just became our way of life. It's crazy and a bit ridiculous to think that you always have to look over your shoulder, but you do.

*

In 2012, while the targeted bullying and harassment by protestors toward me continued, and after much huffing and puffing on my part, I finally got PPRM to agree to do a security audit of the places I worked regularly, because the protestors started following me everywhere I went. A couple times a week I would have to go to other Planned Parenthood health centers, and the protestors started tagging along. I was uncomfortable. What were they up to? What's the endgame? Why follow—basically stalk—someone?

PPRM hired an external security company to audit our safety setup at work. When the results came back, it included some pretty basic things as well as some other suggestions that were more involved and expensive. Immediately following the audit, our security director at the time walked out with no notice. He simply put his badge and phone in a manila envelope and dropped it in his boss's mail folder. He didn't even say he was leaving. The truth is, in the end, nothing ever happened with the suggestions that came out of that security audit. Nothing changed.

Looking back now, it seems crazy that these weren't bigger red flags of impending doom. I was a squeaky wheel, though. I brought security issues to the attention of both local and national Planned Parenthoods whenever they came up. I continued to improve my security tips and tricks for the physicians and providers who were under me at the time so that we could all feel safe. For instance, my husband and I created and presented two different PowerPoint presentations. One was for new physicians coming into PP; we strongly feel that initiating proactive safety steps, rather than trying to put Band-Aids in place after these domestic terrorists descend on you, is the best way to play an active role in one's personal safety.

The other presentation was called *Managing Online Vulnerabilities,* and it basically walked through the various means by which one's address or identifying information can be found on the Internet. Additionally, we trained them to take actions such as setting up Google alerts and making connections with local law enforcement in order to collaboratively plan how to handle protestors showing up at your home. Luckily, we had done this years before it happened, so when we called our local police to relay what was happening in the wake of all these fake videos, it took just minutes to pull together everything we needed to keep our community safe.

Some of us even developed a small support group outside of work, called Stand Strong, that met once or twice a month to share resources and talk openly about juggling work and our anxieties over safety. As a group, we wrote some template letters that we could have on hand in case we ever needed them. We wanted to be prepared because we knew that it was tough to pull things together when in crisis. Ironically, one of those letters served as the framework for my e-mail to neighbors that is included at the beginning of this book.

So here we stood, my husband and I. The potential for extremist protestors to engage in bad behavior seemed so clear to us, and yet the local and national Planned Parenthood authorities and security experts simply dismissed us again and again. Nevertheless, we continued to talk to colleagues about safety and security, especially once we saw that the protestors really had no boundaries. No law was going to save me. The police were helpful, but there were limits to what could legally be done. Protestors were following me from the main Planned Parenthood site to other locations. We figured that at some point, they would follow me home.

CHAPTER 3

THE INFILTRATION

OUR TWIN BOYS were born in the summer of 2014. I took them everywhere with me. Even if I had to travel for work, my husband and I did our best to make sure they could come along. I never wanted to be apart from them.

I headed to a work conference in Miami in October 2014 with the babies. It was our first trip as a family, and the boys were not even four months old. Needless to say, it took careful planning and coordinating on our part. My parents even met us there to help with childcare while I attended the conference and my husband attended to his daytime work duties.

Conferences like this were a standard routine in my professional life at the time, and I looked forward to the same two conferences every year. Physicians, mid-level providers, medical and administrative staff, and anyone and everyone connected to the world of family planning attended these conferences year after year to learn about new technology, interesting research, and opportunities for collaborative work, as well as to network and connect with others in our field. Our conferences were considered "safe" spaces; they were promised to us as precisely that.

One element of being at these conferences involves walking around the exhibit hall and chatting with exhibitors and networking. At this specific conference, the national branch of Planned Parenthood—the Planned Parenthood Federation of America (PPFA)—had encouraged us ahead of time to meet with a company called Biomax Procurement Services. Apparently, they were offering a unique opportunity for those of us who were involved in clinical research. Biomax was headed up by someone named Robert Sarkis— which, as we later learned, was one of David Daleiden's fake names (in the chapters to come, I will refer to him as David).

We were told that the company, Biomax, worked in fetal-tissue research. PPFA said this was a new opportunity they hoped that any of us interested in clinical research would take the time to learn more about. Generally speaking, researchers use fetal tissue because it is an invaluable resource for undifferentiated cells, which can be used to study treatments and cures for many diseases and conditions—including Alzheimer's, diabetes, macular degeneration, and HIV/AIDS.

I spoke to David briefly at the conference and was vaguely intrigued. I wanted to learn more about the research he was talking about. I had never done any work in fetal-tissue research myself, and I was open to learning more. The potential for treatments and cures for the many conditions that plagued so many people close to me in and of itself sparked my intrigue, let alone the tremendous potential impact on public health.

I feel that an immense amount of good comes out of research and clinical trials. I do not have an ethical dilemma about this. I have always been a curious person. In fact, a large part of what I wanted to spend my time on when I began my career as a doctor was clinical research.

But back in October of 2014, at the conference in Miami, the simplest way to explain my state of mind was that I was dead tired. I wasn't getting any sleep; I was working full time, I was a new mom, and our twins were just about four months old. Need I say more?

David's company and learning about the research opportunity they were offering just wasn't a priority for me at the time. I had a five-minute conversation with him in which I basically said, "Who are you guys? What is this research opportunity about? Here's my card."

I had a couple of friends and colleagues with me at the time of the conversation. The real irony here is that I'm actually not a person who regularly goes into exhibit halls to meet with exhibitors. I will sometimes show up to get coffee or chocolate, or say hello to someone I know, but I generally don't enter the exhibit halls looking to buy equipment or talk to vendors. However, on this particular day, I went in to have a quick drive-by chat with David—and that was all it took for the dominoes to start to fall. After my initial brief interaction with David, I returned to Denver and connected my clinical research coordinator with his team to follow up.

I had no reason to find David suspicious. Did I think he

was a little odd? Yes, I did. Nevertheless, I sure didn't expect that five-minute conversation to significantly alter the trajectory of my life. Yet, it did.

*

After we returned from the conference in Miami, David pushed for a meeting right away. I still had too much going on between work and motherhood; my kids weren't even sleeping through the night yet. I advised my research coordinator that I didn't have brain space to engage in further discussion about this opportunity until the following year. In hindsight, I am so thankful that the exhaustion of parenting combined with my professional workload delayed my interaction with David and his fake company. In January of 2015, we agreed to set up a phone call with David and his team. I recall the conversation as having been fairly general. We asked questions about what Biomax did, how they did it, and what this opportunity entailed.

Though we discussed clinical research, the logistics we spoke about during the call were not only foreign to me, they also weren't making any sense. For one, I had never previously had an intermediary working between me and another researcher. Plus, I hadn't done much tissue research of any kind, let alone fetal tissue research. But when I did—for example, when I engaged in a clinical study on preeclampsia—I worked directly with the researcher. It was always researcher to researcher.

I had a hard time comprehending how David's company worked. Frankly, I didn't understand what their purpose was, and honestly, they didn't seem to have much depth to their knowledge. I recall telling my coordinator that the conversation with Biomax seemed recurrently circular; that should have been my big red flag, *but* PPFA had blessed these folks, this company, this opportunity. So I asked my coordinator and myself what Biomax brought to the table. Why wouldn't we just work directly with a researcher?

Another key point: I'm not an embryologist. I'm a physician, yes—but embryology is not my specialty. During the phone call, I also remember feeling concerned about who would take responsibility for identifying different organs for the researcher.

These were my immediate reactions.

As we got to talking about pricing, it felt to me like they functioned as an intermediary so that *they* could make money off of this process. This really was not sitting well with me. Something didn't ring true about what Biomax was trying to "sell" to us. It felt like they weren't completely making sense, and my main question was *"Why do we need you?"*

Then they asked us for a copy of the contract we used for the preeclampsia maternal-placenta-tissue research study. We said we could probably show them parts of it, but that generally, we needed to get things redacted through our lawyers first.

In return, we asked them for an example of a contract they had used before so that we could learn more about what they were presenting—and ultimately make an educated decision about whether or not this opportunity was something in which we wanted to participate. I remember David sort of stumbling over that particular request, but we didn't have any real reason to be concerned about this. I also felt like we didn't need to make any decisions on that call. We just asked them to send us material and information for our review.

When we received the sample contract from David, we gave it to our PPRM lawyer and told him that we were potentially interested in this research opportunity, but we didn't really know a whole lot about it.

He looked through it and basically said, "What the hell is this?" He redlined the whole thing. He said the contracts were crappy and that if we were going to move forward, that they would have to fix all of it. In other words, we were not going to do anything the way David and Biomax had it written in the contracts they provided.

Looking back now, of course, we know that the contracts they sent were complete bullshit. They had just slapped them together. They had never done any real work before because Biomax was a front; it was a fake company collecting data and information to create fake news.

Anytime I do research, one of the most important things my coordinator and I do is try to evaluate and vet how the research logistics will work within our current system. We asked David and his team a lot of questions about how things would work. For one, we didn't have any embryologists on staff. We needed more information. And *that* is when they finagled an in-person visit.

They said, "Why don't we come see your facilities? We'll see how things go, and we can talk about the logistics. Then we'll be able to better define how this could work in your system." So we agreed.

For context, it's common for us to take meetings like this for clinical-research opportunities; it's a normal part of our routine. With some of the medications and technologies pharmaceutical companies are trying to get approved these days, it's almost once a month that someone comes in for a general meeting like this. They usually come and visit with us first, and then the research doesn't begin for another six to eight months. A lot of planning is involved. We check off a lot of boxes first: review protocols, define internal logistics, complete regulatory and ethics committee paperwork, and then plan to train everyone who might be involved.

*

In April, David and his colleague came to the PPRM headquarters for our meeting. A normal research team visit concerning our possible participation in a research opportunity would have included materials for us to review together and checklists of requirements for our facility to qualify as a research trial site. Someone from the company usually works closely with our clinical research coordinator prior to the visit to review requirements and to help us prepare for the visit. Nothing even close to that happened with Biomax. Right off the bat, upon their arrival onsite at PPRM, the Biomax team made some missteps.

First, they showed up about twenty minutes late for the meeting. Then, after the late arrival, David spent almost ten minutes fiddling with his phone. During their visit, Sandra Merritt—who posed as Biomax's CEO using false credentials and the fake name Susan Tennenbaum—accidentally called "Robert Sarkis" by his real name, David. It was all "off," and within minutes of starting our meeting my goal was to wrap this up and get on with my day as quickly as I could.

I thought it was all a little odd and highly unprofessional. David's preoccupation with whatever was going on with his phone actually started to border on flat-out rudeness. We were trying to get our meeting started, and there he was, fiddling with his phone and not saying a word about what he was doing or what was going on.

I realize now that he must have been having trouble with whatever app was connected to the hidden camera he was wearing—trying to turn it on or something. I remember saying something along the lines of "Do you need time to finish whatever you're doing before we begin?"

One positive is that because I happened to be sitting in a part of the room where the sun was really bright behind me, you can't see me well in part of the video because I'm backlit. This was a small victory.

Another odd thing that happened that morning is that I had an intern with me that day, and I asked her to sit in on the meeting with us. This was pretty common. She was a very bright high school student who wanted to go into medicine—or maybe even medical law. This intern had been working with me for almost a year at that point. Before the meeting, I told her that it was a new endeavor, and she should sit in on the meeting and listen. "I'm learning myself," I told her.

Because she was in the meeting, I introduced her to David and his fake CEO and explained that she was sitting in because this is one way I try to broaden the experience of my interns and help students learn and engage.

I asked, "Can you tell her a little bit about how you became interested in the work that you are doing? How did you got involved in this line of work? What schooling and career path got you to where you are now?"

I think the whole line of questioning completely threw them off. They both came up with some really pathetic backstories. I remember thinking, *Seriously, that doesn't make any sense at all. That's not helpful for her, or really, any of us.* I recall David sharing some cockamamie story about a cousin, which didn't even make sense; it was just a jumble of words. I lost some respect for him right there.

I had set aside about an hour for the meeting. Normally when people come in to discuss research opportunities, they have lots of logistics and details to talk through. Sometimes they have PowerPoint presentations to show us. In other words, they come prepared. This was not at all the case in this meeting. I ended up cutting this one short because there were these long, awkward pauses throughout. I found myself repeating the same questions over and over again, and their answers to my questions didn't make sense.

I thought to myself, *Boy, I'm going to have to reach out to other colleagues who are already involved in this work. I'm going to have to get more information about engaging in this type of research and this Biomax company because what these people are saying isn't making any logical sense.* The only reason I was even continuing to court the opportunity was because the Planned Parenthood national office had promoted it.

Based on how the meeting went, I began to lose interest in David and the opportunity. It didn't sound like they had it all together. I have since spent countless hours—days, even—thinking back on these interactions with David and Biomax. As I recount it for you here, I can't believe I didn't pick up on it or act on all the red flags that were presenting themselves to me. Maybe it was because I was a bit exhausted by the combination of infant twins and a hectic work schedule. In the back of my mind and in my gut, during every interaction with them, it felt like something was wrong or "off." They never had solid, reasonable answers for me, and they didn't seem to know what they were doing. But while I made my best effort to remain professional, interested, and civil, I was hoping this encounter would end quickly, as this discussion wasn't going anywhere. Every single time I was around them, something inside me would tell me to leave—not just to walk away, but to *run*.

And while we never agreed to move forward with them after that meeting—no contracts were ever signed; no plans were put in place—it was already too late. The damage was done. They had the footage they needed to concoct fake news and inflict real damage.

*

After our meeting, I went to see some patients and David and his fake CEO stayed on to discuss "logistics" with my coordinator. The plan was for them to come back to the lab area to observe our post-procedure process. This way, we could continue to talk about the research work they were proposing and my coordinator and I could observe David's supposed skill and knowledge about his work.

I left them and performed a couple of procedures. When we evacuate the uterus, the contents go into these containers that our nurses then process. We aim to prevent any disturbance for the patient and we want to keep things as respectful and private as possible. I then finish up with my patient while one nurse or support staff processes the tissue. By the time I take my leave of my patient with one nurse, another nurse has processed the material in the lab so that I can look at it and confirm that the procedure was successful.

However, this time, when I went back into the lab area, David and Susan were back there with my coordinator. Mind you, we were under the impression that David was an expert in fetal-tissue research. That's what they'd told us their company did. I could sense that Susan was uncomfortable and wanted to get out of the area as quickly as possible; her discomfort was almost palpable. She excused herself and left the room to go "take care of something."

What happened next was truly bizarre.

David put on gloves, and although I don't believe this was shown in the video, my recollection is that I saw him put his fingers right in there with the tissue. There was something overzealous about his actions, like he was enjoying the experience too much—so much so that it no longer appeared professional or appropriate. It reminded me of how kids get excited when they have sensory playtime and they're allowed to put their hands in a pile of dried beans or Play-Doh. David though, appeared to be having fun playing in *fetal tissue*. It was gross and disrespectful.

I distinctly remember him having a smile on this face at one point; I was both perplexed and put off. *Who is this guy?* I thought. *How creepy is he, and what the hell is going on?* And I am speaking as someone who has done this work for a long time. I am very comfortable working with tissue. But something about the way he touched it made the hair on the back of my neck stand up.

Now that I know who David really is, it is clear that he is deeply disturbed. It was evident in the zeal with which he physically manipulated the tissue. To this day, I still shudder thinking about it.

I've thought a lot about what he was doing in that period of time in which he was wearing gloves, and why. One theory is that because he had small hands, perhaps he was trying to make it look like they were *my* hands manipulating the tissue in the video.

He filmed our entire meeting. Based on the footage that was later released, it's likely that his video camera was either hidden in his glasses or in one of his shirt's buttonholes.

I think the tissue part of the video was what the public had the strongest reaction to, and I get it. I can completely understand how seeing tissue like that, without context and in a video purposefully edited to be dramatic, could be upsetting. Bear in mind that human tissue, mucus, blood, organs, and poop are things that many physicians see regularly—daily, even. But a layperson watching that video might have been completely caught off guard, shocked, even disgusted. But that *was* David's goal. He sensationalized it.

This is a highly sensitive and personal matter for our patients. As physicians, we are very aware of that sensitivity and try to be respectful of it. I have patients who, for a lot of different reasons, want to take their tissue home with them after the termination. Sometimes people want to have some type of ceremony or a funeral, or do something else that is symbolic and meaningful for them.

Often, patients just want to physically see the tissue after the procedure. And I completely support their decision, as long as they're aware of what they are going to see. Some people seem better prepared than others. In the circumstance that a patient asks to see the material after I have left the room, my nurses make sure to explain to them that they can't unsee things, and take time to talk about being prepared for what they are asking to see. I view it as a privilege, an honor, to have helped this woman through her experience.

With early-stage procedures, I think it can be a great learning experience for patients if—and only if—they ask to see their pregnancy. This way, they can see that anti-abortion rhetoric about the pregnancy looking like a "real baby" is completely inaccurate. In an early-stage procedure, I think the pregnancy material really looks more like a cloud; it's a puffy ball.

That's why the words that David dubbed into the videos is so absurd. They added in phrases like "that's brains" and "It's a baby." It wasn't brains, and that isn't terminology a physician would ever use. A resident who was working with me the day of the filming had some other phrase assigned to her, like, "And another boy!" It's not only completely untrue; it is unrealistic.

I was unsettled by the entire encounter with David and his "CEO." After the meeting, I e-mailed a few colleagues to get some general information about how research like this would even work in our facility.

I said we were generally interested in learning more about fetal-tissue research—having nothing to do with David or his company, Biomax—and asked them things like, "How do you guys do this? What are the rules? How do you make it work?"

Because of the experience during our office meeting, I wasn't overly impressed with Biomax or David himself. We had a bunch of other things going on at the time, and I remember telling my coordinator that this was not high on my list of priorities. I didn't feel we needed to actively pursue it.

But after a while, my coordinator needed to check things off his list. He came to me and asked, "Can we just come up with a yes or no here so that I can take it off my list?" Otherwise, it would just end up being one of those things that's still awaiting a response.

He eventually followed up with David and they e-mailed us this bizarre list of things that they said "everybody was looking for." Someone wanted a liver—and something else like that. There was some strange language in the e-mail, and again, a lot of it didn't make sense to me.

Looking back, it's really too bad that we hadn't e-mailed them something like, "Thanks for coming up to visit us, but we're not interested. This is just not for us right now."

We didn't do that because—now, I realize—I was trying too hard to be nice. I was giving them a chance to respond even though we had way too much on our collective plate.

We didn't interact with them again from early May until July. A follow-up e-mail was sent in early July and we never heard back from them. The videos came out the following week.

CHAPTER 4

A SHITSTORM'S COMING

JULY 14, 2015.

I went into work and remember it being a pretty normal day. My twins were just over a year old. They were at home with our nanny. I was in my office at work, preparing for the day. As I was opening and reading my snail mail, my e-mail dinged, signaling a new message.

It was an e-mail from PPRM CEO Vicki. I remember reading the subject line: *Heads up — Live Action Operation happening now.*

I quickly scanned through the rest of the message, and when I came to the words *They created a fake organization: Biomax,* I felt my gut drop. I wrote back right away and told Vicki that they were here, in our offices—that I had met with them and they had met with some of our staff. I basically said, and I knew deep in my core, *Get ready. A shitstorm's coming.*

In that moment, all the creepy feelings I had about David and our interactions came into crystal-clear focus.

I realized why things hadn't made sense before: the whole enterprise was fake, a ruse.

The security concerns hadn't even hit me yet, as things were moving so fast. I called my husband right away. This is one of the things we had been worried about; it was something we had been planning for. This was the exact type of scenario that concerned us when we noticed the protesters getting more and more specific over the past few years. I told him what had happened. I told him that David had been to my office and now they likely had a video with me in it.

That morning, the PPRM communications director came into my office and said, "Hey, can you take a look at this video with me?"

I'm sure I looked at her like a deer in headlights.

She continued, "The video turns my stomach. Everyone's pretty disgusted."

The video in question had been released by the Center for Medical Progress—David Daleiden's anti-choice organization—and featured a California Planned Parenthood physician named Deborah Nucatola. It appeared to be an older conversation between David and Deborah, filmed during a lunch meeting. We later learned that the video had been recorded at some point in 2013, before I had met David.

Deborah had been with Planned Parenthood for many years and, at the time, she also held a pretty major position at the national office. Based on what was said in the video, at face value, it looked pretty bad. The conversation was held in a public place, and it showed her talking about things that without proper context seem inappropriate.

The communications director stood over me at my computer as I watched the video. It became apparent right away that Planned Parenthood was taking the conversation at face value. In other words, they didn't have any reason to think that words had been spliced into or deleted from the conversation. Their immediate internal interpretation of the video was that it was a completely inappropriate conversation. The communications director asked me what I thought.

I told her that I felt bad for Deb. I felt horrible that someone whose sole intention is to help women was getting skewered internally and externally all because of internal judgment and someone else's ideology. Obviously, David was steering conversations in a direction that would lead to pretty specific detail, which he could then place wildly out of context. But that doesn't mean we don't have these types of conversations about procedure, techniques, or skills with colleagues. Sometimes we talk about aspects of a procedure that might be challenging, or we discuss circumstances that make things more complicated. Physicians, just like many other professionals, have conversations about technique and skill, particularly as it relates to managing challenges and unanticipated events. This is not abnormal or inappropriate.

Even though I am trained in these procedures and have performed them for years, it doesn't mean that they are always easy. Some people think this is heartless work, when, in fact, *it isn't*. A lot of it becomes routine over time, but there are moments even within that realm that, for whatever reason, there are unanticipated challenges, or the situation itself just makes one pause.

I had a patient not too long ago who was barely a teenager. It was a rape case. Situations like this absolutely break my heart. As providers, we look outside at the protesters and want to say, "You're going to call *us* disgusting? You protestors are the ones videotaping and yelling at patients entering or exiting the clinic that you are going to post a video of them on Facebook or YouTube, and 'make them famous' for having their abortion!" I see myself as someone helping a woman who has made a choice, a choice that she can legally make, and I have the privilege of helping her get back on her path. That is nothing short of an honor for me.

*

The day that first video was released, everyone at Planned Parenthood mobilized—nationally and locally. People started raising their hands and saying, "They were *here* too." It was like a wave of hands raising across Planned Parenthoods all around the country saying, "They were here. I talked to them." David had participated in conversations with a lot of providers, either at conferences or over drinks. Conducting in-person meetings with providers at Planned Parenthood facilities was a less common practice of his, thankfully, but I knew I fell into that unlucky group.

The worst part was knowing that they had been *here with us*—that they had been allowed through the doors. I knew it was just a matter of time until my video came out. I had so many questions. *What were they going to show? What was it going to look like?* I knew they were going to cast me in the worst light possible and take many things out of context. *Oh my God.*

I felt sick to my stomach and didn't quite know what to do with myself. All I could do was try to recall every little last thing from deep within my memory. I was trying to remember anything that might've slipped my mind over the last nine months. I needed to put it all together and organize it. I felt like we needed to throw everything up on a whiteboard and look at exactly what we were up against.

I was very up-front with Planned Parenthood from the start. I told them about every interaction I'd had with David. I didn't want to withhold anything, so I told them exactly what had happened in the best detail that I could.

My dad always talked about honesty, both as an individual and as a doctor. Very early on in my medical career, he reminded me, explicitly, never to lie about anything. And I have always been up-front—even as a little kid. If I got caught doing something wrong, I would always fess up and say, "Yes, I did it." I wouldn't lie. I wasn't good at it because it never felt right to me. Then there is David Daleiden, who knowingly built a house of cards based on lies.

I spent the rest of that day in meetings trying to figure out what happened—talking to the national office and telling them about David's visit to PPRM.

After people spoke to Deborah directly and re-watched

the video, it became clear that this wasn't just a video. It was a *spliced-and-diced* video; it was fake. This made the whole thing even scarier because then we knew they were heavily editing the footage. This was alarming because it meant that they could create their own narrative—even if that meant completely making things up.

*

Three days after Deborah's video was released, Planned Parenthood made the following public statement:

> *"Planned Parenthood of the Rocky Mountains does not participate in fetal tissue donations and flatly denies ever altering a procedure for the purpose of organ or tissue retrieval.*

"Patients sometimes want to donate tissue to scientific research that can help lead to medical breakthroughs, such as treatments and cures for serious diseases. Women at Planned Parenthood who have abortions are no different. Several Planned Parenthood health centers around the country help patients who want to donate tissue for scientific research—with full, informed consent from patients and in full compliance with ethical and legal standards. There is no financial benefit for tissue donation for either the patient or for Planned Parenthood. In some instances, actual costs, such as the cost to transport tissue to leading research centers, are reimbursed, which is standard across the medical field."[2]

*

But things got nasty. Quickly. Social media was blowing up. In the days following her video release, I later learned that Deborah Nucatola had received death threats and possibly even had a bounty placed on her head. As a result, she'd had a US Marshal and armed security assigned to her.

I sat at home and waited. I couldn't sleep, as my brain was churning. I needed to do something.

On July 20, 2015—six days after the first video came out—I felt I needed to write to my staff and colleagues at PPRM. I was trying to be proactive. I wanted to prepare them for what was to come.

I sent an e-mail to my colleagues across PPRM. In that communication I acknowledged that I had unknowingly invited these anti-abortion extremists into PPRM in my quest to support scientific research. I explained that fetal tissue research had played an essential role in the development of vaccines for polio, rubella, and measles, and that it is essential for identifying life-saving treatments for conditions such as cancer, Alzheimer's, Parkinson's, and retinal disease.

I reminded my colleagues that many of our patients

---

2   "Statement from Planned Parenthood on New Under-
      cover Video," Planned Parenthood press release, https://www.
      plannedparenthood.org/about-us/newsroom/press-releases/
      statement-from-planned-parenthood-on-new-undercover-video

requested that their fetal tissue be donated for scientific research. For these patients, this donation was a way to do something positive or contribute to something bigger than themselves during a difficult time. This was yet another reason I had engaged David: I was trying to learn more about something my patients frequently requested and that we currently did not offer.

I explained that the main goal of this infiltration was to promote their anti-abortion agenda, vilify me as an abortion provider, and ultimately eliminate access to safe abortion. Most important, I wanted to prepare my colleagues for what I knew was coming: they needed to understand that I had been covertly recorded, that the videos had been grossly edited to show many of us saying things or behaving in a manner likely to cause the public to question our ethics, morals, professionalism, and lawfulness.

I did not want the staff to second-guess the importance of our work or to doubt my true intentions. I wanted them to feel confident and remain steadfast in their efforts to ensure that women had access to safe, professional health care, despite the risks they all took.

I went on to describe how I had been recorded without my awareness, and therefore, though I had been professional, I was relatively casual and unguarded. Thus I was vulnerable, just as anyone would be if they thought they were having conversations in a safe place with colleagues.

I pre-emptively apologized for anything they were going to see or hear that might make them uncomfortable. I knew that videos involving me were forthcoming, and I knew they were going to be horrible, judging from the edited videos David had already released. I invited my colleagues to engage me in open conversation about any of this.

My communication was very well received, and my colleagues enthusiastically rallied around me and around Planned Parenthood, without hesitation.

It turned out that my timing with this e-mail was just right. My video was released the following week. But first came Dr. Mary Gatter.

*

July 21, 2015.

David Daleiden and the Center for Medical Progress released their second "undercover" video one week after the first. This video featured Dr. Mary Gatter, who, at the time, was a Planned Parenthood medical director. She is the one who quickly became known as the Lamborghini Lady because of a joke she made. Almost instantly, she was a hashtag on Twitter.

But she was only joking. Mary has a very dry sense of humor, and this was merely an example of that, but David spliced that line into the video to make it look like she would be open to selling fetal body parts for profit.

The full video shows her talking about fetal-tissue donation and the processing costs—all of which are legal. While the discussion about dollar amounts in the conversation may sound alarming, small payments for transportation and processing are legal in human fetal-tissue donation.

Under 42 US Code § 289g–2, the law allows for "reasonable payments associated with the transportation, implantation, processing, preservation, quality control, or storage of human fetal tissue."

In fact, you actually hear Mary say, "We're not in it for the money," and "We don't want to be in the position of being accused of selling tissue." But the fallout from this second video was extreme. It was all over Twitter and Facebook. There were hashtags, memes, nasty quotes, and horrible e-mail messages being circulated. Dr. Gatter quickly got armed security assigned to her as well because of threats on Twitter. Everyone was upset.

I had to notify the parents of the intern who was with me during the meeting with David because she was a minor. My coordinator was anxious and worried about his family. Everyone was on edge.

*

In the beginning—when these first two videos came out—it felt like a war room at work. We were all in it together. It was like we'd had the rug pulled out from underneath us, all at once. Everyone was sitting together, debriefing, and saying things like, "We can do this," and "We're going to get through it together."

There wasn't a lot of blame being thrown around yet.

Everyone was just so frazzled and surprised. We were all trying to do the right thing. I didn't quite know how things were going to unfold. Then—as time went on and the fog lifted—of course people started pointing fingers and blaming.

Then there was the longstanding history of my husband and me going to Planned Parenthood and pushing for an appropriate level of security, and always feeling like no one was taking us seriously. To get caught up in it all myself now—well, it was shocking.

I knew something was coming. I felt this inescapable sense of impending doom. It was worse not knowing the how and the when. *What were they going to do? How? When?* I fell asleep only at the point of exhaustion those nights, asking myself how and when.

After seeing how badly Dr. Nucatola had been judged, I was paralyzed with fear. I wasn't sure how they were going to edit and splice my video, but I never imagined that they could take it a level beyond that. What could be worse than editing and splicing? Adding in words that I never said.

CHAPTER 5

FRONT AND CENTER

JULY 28, 2015.

David's group released their videos slowly at first—once a week, on Tuesdays. First, it was Dr. Deborah Nucatola. Then, Dr. Mary Gatter. Tuesday had become my least favorite day, one that I always began following a sleepless night coupled with anxiety.

On Tuesday, July 28, 2015, I got an early-morning text from my communications director. Amid all the chaos, we'd struck a deal once the fake video release started: if anything new happened—especially if it involved me—she would let me know right away.

I read the words on my phone: *New video released today. You are in it.*

I fell to my knees in my living room and heard the words, "Oh my God" tumble out of my mouth as if somebody else had spoken them.

My husband heard me and came in quickly from the other room. We had just woken up; it was early, and the babies were still asleep. He picked me up off the floor, and I showed him my phone.

My husband took out his laptop and searched for the video; within a few moments he had found it. I heard some of the audio but couldn't bring myself to watch it. I had to leave the room.

It felt like my heart had dropped deep down into my stomach. Of course, I knew I had never engaged in fetal-tissue research. I knew that David Daleiden had a personal agenda, and that he was attempting to use me as just one of his pawns to push that agenda forward. I knew that everything in the video would be lies.

My husband watched the whole thing and did his best to be supportive, but he was completely wrecked by how I was portrayed in it. I remember tears of frustration and helplessness welling up in his eyes as he held my hand. We looked at each other, and one of us said, "What the fuck just happened?" There was just one other question on both of our minds: *What now?*

Within a manner of minutes, my world had imploded. Everything felt hazy. I was stunned—dazed, actually. I saw the faces of different people in my life pop up on a rotating screen inside my mind: my parents, my mother-in-law, my sister, her son, all of my friends. Everyone.

Would they understand? Would they know this wasn't real? So many people (including many smart people and even some of the media) had been fooled by this video. *How do I even begin to communicate? What do we do?* I thought about our twins sleeping in the other room. Everything passed by me in a blur. I don't know how long I stared off into space or at the white wall in front of me. I don't remember everything my husband said.

Ironically, just a couple of weeks before, we had enjoyed a great family weekend over the Fourth of July. It had been peaceful and full of hope. I remember looking over at my husband and saying, "Wow, look at us. We have one-year-old twins!"

My work had been going pretty well. We'd refinanced the house and were planning to get it paid down so we could eventually sell it in order to get into a place that would have more space for the twins. We had made it over some of the big hurdles, and it felt like we could start focusing on the *future*. It felt as if everything was finally lining up—and then it just came crashing down right there in that moment. With one text. With one click on a screen. Because of one false prophet—a liar, and a man without honor, named David Daleiden.

The video featured me and some woman, a hired actor, who said she worked in fetal-tissue research. On camera, they had her talk about "killing babies," and what the process was like. I heard bits and pieces of it and thought about what a liar she was. I couldn't focus. I didn't care to watch the videos in their entirety. I know more about the videos because of what I've been told and from snippets I've been forced to watch to deliver my perspective and recollection of what really happened versus the sensationalized fiction that David created. My forehead felt hot. I was furious.

The good news was that most of the video focused on the paid actor, and in fact, it was pretty monotonous compared to the other videos that had come before it. They cut to me a little bit in this one, but there weren't many damaging statements attributed to me. Of course, I knew this was only the beginning. I was still all over Twitter—memes, hashtags, you name it. An image flashed into my mind of David in our lab with those gloves on, molesting the tissue in such a sick way. I shook my head as if to erase it from my memory.

✳

My husband and I pulled ourselves together that morning— because we *had* to. That's what you do. My little babies were going to be waking up soon and I needed to be strong and resilient. I needed to protect them from this horror. I didn't want to have any negative energy with which to greet them when they awoke with their goofy grins and warm cuddles. They didn't deserve it. They needed their mama whole, happy, strong, and solid. We knew the day would be hard, but that we would have to get through it. I needed to get to the office and start to figure things out; we needed a game plan. I was starting to get calls from colleagues.

I am comfortable in a crisis. I have always had one mantra when faced with a challenge: no matter what, minutes turn into hours; hours, into days; days, into weeks, and so on, so I never rush. I trust that solutions, paths forward, the best decisions will make themselves apparent to me. They always have, and yet again, they will now. I'm accustomed to working under pressure because of my medical training; like everyone, I've had my share of life's curveballs and challenges. The world keeps spinning, right? The river always flows.

The babies were going to wake up soon, and the nanny was coming. We had to get to work.

Hours later, I received a call from the new national Planned Parenthood office's chief medical officer, who had been hired just weeks before this scandal. Talk about timing! During the course of our conversation, she asked us to please share the security tips that my husband and I had worked on. I couldn't believe it. My life was disintegrating before my eyes. I was trying to figure out how to talk to my family, friends, and colleagues, and now I was on the phone with the new chief medical officer and she was asking *me* for security tips?!

I wanted to scream, "This is what the national office should've been doing in the first place!" But, of course, I didn't do that. I couldn't.

Instead, I sent her the PowerPoint we had created, and a list of the most important safety recommendations. I was hoping that at least the information could help others.

I told her, "Here is where you can start. I'll be happy to deal with this when the storm is over." I had more important things to attend to at the moment.

Because two other videos had been released before mine, Planned Parenthood was already developing a process for dealing with this type of bogus material. They needed support, and so they'd hired a PR company to help.

This was the way it went: David's Center for Medical Progress would release a video. The media would then pick it up, and the Internet would go crazy. Hours or days later, the Center for Medical Progress would release what they called the "full videos." These "full videos" were sometimes three or four hours long.

It would often take Planned Parenthood and the PR team *days* to transcribe the multi-hour videos. They would have a team of people transcribe the videos and then compare the transcripts of the first version to the "full videos." Often, the transcripts wouldn't line up.

In fact, the Center for Medical Progress would post their own version of a transcript next to each of their videos, and even *those* wouldn't match our transcripts. They would chop things out for whatever reason. It was difficult to keep track. This was all on purpose, of course. It made it impossible for anyone to know the truth.

By the time we had finished transcribing the first full video, the second one was already out. It was a constant game of catch-up.

My first video was released on Tuesday, July 28, 2015. But instead of waiting until the following Tuesday as usual, they released my second video just two days later, on July 30, 2015. This video was their gold mine.

I was featured much more prominently this time, and the video was much more graphic. It showed things that people were not used to seeing. It was shocking and devastating. That's when things went from bad to worse.

I remember calling my therapist and saying that I needed to come in right away. This was not a new therapist—I knew him, and he knew me—but when I saw him, it felt like even *he* had become skeptical of me once he'd viewed that second video. That's how bad it looked. I felt sick to my stomach.

The day my second video came out was supposed to be a travel day for me, but Planned Parenthood pulled me out of the trip because they felt it wasn't safe. People had taken to Twitter, and the reaction to the video was huge. My full name and picture were out there. By now, I had received multiple hashtags, memes, taunts, judgments, and serious death threats. PPFA and Vicki called to inform me that I was getting armed security because of how badly it was going in the press.

They hired a security company, and we had someone outside our house 24/7 just to make sure that there wasn't any kind of "action" occurring. That was the word they used.

Luckily, my husband and I had had the foresight years before to use a PO box instead of our home address for our mail. We didn't want our house to be so easily identifiable. Because of this, when the videos first came out, we did not have people crowding around our home in protest of me—at least, not yet.

But I had made one big mistake with David Daleiden: I'd given him my business card at that meeting in Miami. My work phone number and e-mail address were on that card—and he'd included these in the video, of course. It was just one more way for him to place a bull's-eye on my head and put my family in danger.

As a result, I was soon flooded with e-mail and voicemail messages. I've saved some of them in an e-mail folder labeled "Attacks." The work phone calls and voicemail messages got so bad that I told my boss to shut down the phone line. I received e-mail messages from people all over the world, telling me that I was a terrible person. People even started contacting me on LinkedIn.

One of those messages was the one that called me "a fucking monster who sells crushed babies," the one from the person who wanted to nominate me as a "top 100 evil person of 2015"—a competition I hadn't even known existed.

But I was most shocked when my brother-in-law (someone we thought would never be so easily fooled by a fake video) posted the video on Facebook. It was just heartbreaking. My parents, on the other hand, have always been fully supportive of what I do; however, I don't think they ever grasped the kind of danger I was in as a provider. They were always proud of my work and my accomplishments, and my aunts and uncles felt the same way. As a family, we were pro-choice. Everyone should have accurate information with which they can make personal decisions that they should not have to defend to anyone else.

But then Bill O'Reilly featured my video on his show. That's when my parents started hearing from their friends. Someone called them and said, "Hey, Savita is on TV."

O'Reilly's segment—called "Is America Becoming Barbaric?"—began like this: "Today, pro-life Americans in more than fifty cities protested against Planned Parenthood after gruesome undercover videos showed the organization selling the organs of dead babies."

A sound byte from Senator Ted Cruz flashed on the screen: "Today the US Department of Justice should open a criminal investigation into whether Planned Parenthood nationally is a criminal enterprise breaking the law," he said.

O'Reilly featured some of the footage from one of my fake videos and described me as, "Dr. Savita Ginde, the medical director of Planned Parenthood in Colorado, talking about selling the body parts of a fetus aborted after eleven weeks, six days."

My parents were shocked. There it was, right before their eyes: Bill O'Reilly, saying my name on the air and showing the bogus video to his two million nightly viewers.

My parents called me immediately. I remember my mom crying on the phone. By then, my husband had already spoken with his mother, and she had cried too. Everyone was scared and confused. I was being attacked on national television. My name and photo were everywhere. Words like "baby killer" and "baby parts" were being assigned to me. My name was trending on Twitter.

When I came home from work, we got on the phone with both of our mothers for a family conference call. Everyone was extremely upset. They were scared for us, for our innocent babies. My husband and I hadn't decided what were we going to do yet. What were our options?

We tossed around a bunch of off-the-cuff ideas. Should we run away somewhere for a while and let everything die down? Should we fight back? Did I need a lawyer? What was Planned Parenthood going to do to support us? No one knew what to do. Fortunately (or unfortunately, depending on how you look at it), I'm usually the person in the family who pulls it all together; that's me in a nutshell. But this time, it was so hard. I wanted to fall apart but I couldn't . . . and I didn't.

More than anything, my parents wanted to make sure we were safe. At this point, they'd seen the rhetoric and threats on social media. My sister, whose kid was a teenager at the time, called and said, "Hey, did you know you have a hashtag?" I remember my mom yelling a reminder to me, "You've got kids now!" I was well aware of this fact, of course, and I knew that I had one major job now, just one aim: to protect my children.

Our families were concerned. "How are you going to face this? You have kids. This is not just about you and your career." And believe me, we were all on the same page there.

Priorities became clear very quickly during this time. My husband and I sat down later to make sure we were aligned on everything: *Family first—fuck the job if we need to. Do what we have to do to be safe, and defend ourselves vigorously as necessary.*

*

We tried to slow down over the weekend. My husband and I purposefully kept very quiet over the next few days. We were weighing our options and talking about what to do next.

Our 24/7 security detail remained in front of our house. One afternoon, he noticed a man outside, just casually looking and walking around, like he was trying to scope things out while trying to blend in. Neighbors started asking questions about everything. By then, of course, everyone had seen the news.

When Monday rolled around, I had to go to the office to attempt damage control. I was waiting for the nanny to arrive before I left for work, when our security guy flagged my husband outside.

A woman was taking pictures outside our house. Our nanny arrived at that moment, and when she walked into the house, this woman tried to take pictures through the front door. I think she was trying to get images of me or the kids or the inside of our house. It was odd—both scary and invasive. Our security guard immediately took *her* photo and got one of her CRV's license plate as well. He then approached her and asked who she was and what she was doing there. Appearing flustered, she didn't answer, but rather, rushed to her car and sped away.

At the time we had no idea know who she was. My husband and the security guard immediately began considering the possibilities. She was most likely one of those anti-choice extremists, someone who meant us some kind of harm. But on the other hand, maybe—hopefully—she was a member of the media. But would the media go so far as to take pictures through our front door? The incident concerned our security detail so much that we called national Planned Parenthood and told them what had happened. We informed them that we had a photo of the woman and her license plate.

Instead of jumping into action, they told us that it was a local issue. We were told to go to PPRM about the matter. When we contacted PPRM, they said it could take a week to run the license plate. My husband was in awe of the lack of a sense of urgency, and just said, "Screw 'em. We don't have time for this BS." We called our former and current law-enforcement and private-investigator contacts to give them the information and open a case.

Because of my work at PPRM and my husband's work in security, we had many good contacts at various agencies. We'd always hoped we'd never have to play that card, but we both knew that this was the time. They said they would check the plate and contact us as soon as they had any information.

I went in to work and tried to get some things done, but I couldn't focus. Within an hour, our contact associated with the FBI called me. This whole sequence of events is seared into my brain. I was at work, walking down the steps of the administrative building to the side door that would lead me to my car. The PPRM security director at the time, Robert Beall, was by my side, walking me out. I answered the phone while I was still inside the building. The agent on the line told me that they had obtained the license-plate results, as well as some additional information, and then the line went silent for a moment as she paused. My heart began to pound, and my workbag dropped off my shoulder to the ground.

"This is actually pretty bad," she said. "All I'm going to say is that the woman in front of your house is a major player and a bad actor in the anti-choice movement—and we don't think it is safe for you guys to stay there."

The lady who was taking pictures from every angle outside our home, and who was trying to take pictures of the *inside* of our home through the front door, was Susan Sutherland, a leader at Colorado Right for Life—and apparently someone with a complete disregard for the privacy of others.

I told my security detail that I needed to get home immediately. I felt panicked and anxious. The Mama Bear in me took over and I felt an urgent need to protect my babies.

CHAPTER 6

SAY GOOD-BYE TO YOUR HOME

AUGUST 3, 2015, was the last day I set foot in my home. It was the last time I felt its wood floors beneath my bare feet, the last time my twins played in the bathtub, and the last time my husband turned the lock on the front door.

After receiving the call from the FBI and hearing that we should leave the house immediately, I raced home to my husband and kids. During the drive, I got another phone call. This time it was one of the board members of Colorado's Religious Coalition for Reproductive Choice, an organization that serves as the primary religious voice for reproductive justice in the state. She had seen on the news what was going on, and she was calling to check on me.

My mind was racing, so I blurted it out. I said that we needed to leave our house immediately and asked if she knew anyone with an empty second home. It is common for people in Colorado to have mountain homes, and there were many wealthy people who sat on the board.

We knew we couldn't go to a hotel because we'd been

told not to check in anywhere under our real names. This also ruled out using a service like Airbnb or HomeAway, because our identities could be tracked. My fellow board member said she would make some calls for us.

I got home and held my kids on my lap as my husband and I began to prepare for our exit. I must have done five loads of laundry while we waited to hear if we would have a place to go. We packed up all the things we needed for the babies—bottles, formula, cleaning supplies, and the like. Thankfully, our nanny stayed late to help us.

Finally, while we were folding onesies and packing diapers, we got a call from a different board member who said that she had found a place for us to go.

Our security detail took me directly to the home of our new guardian angels to pick up the keys. My husband stayed behind with the kids and the nanny. When we pulled up to their mansion, I realized I was a complete wreck. I had never met this woman before, but when she opened the door, I just started sobbing right there in front of her. Through my tears, I thanked her over and over again. To this day, every time I think about how selflessly they helped us—complete strangers to them—I still become overwhelmed by emotion.

She gave me the keys, directions to the mountain home, and instructions for turning off the alarm system. My phone buzzed endlessly with a constant stream of texts, e-mail messages, and voicemail messages from colleagues, friends, and neighbors. I couldn't handle it all even though it stemmed from good intentions. Everyone was trying to contact me. I just had to ignore it as much as possible and focus on the safety of my family for now.

Later, we texted a few neighbor friends, telling them that we were leaving and that we would be in touch when we reached our destination. We didn't tell anyone where we were going for safety and security reasons.

Soon afterward, we walked out of our home—just like that.

My husband loaded up his car and drove ahead of me. I followed in my car, with the two babies in back. One security guard led the way and another trailed behind us as we caravanned away from our home. I remember glancing in my rearview mirror as we pulled out of the driveway. It was dark outside, and the weather was warm; it was a perfect summer night in a suddenly imperfect world. It felt ominous to leave in a long procession like that.

We drove all the way out into the mountains, about three hours outside of Denver. One part of that drive has stayed with me to this day; I remember it clearly, even now. I was scared and deeply anxious as I drove along Interstate 70, listening to my kids babbling in the backseat. Of course, they didn't know what the hell was going on. It was around 9:30 at night; they weren't even supposed to be awake.

Tears streamed down my face as I drove with both hands on the wheel. My knuckles were practically white. To get out into the mountains one has to pass through the 1.7-mile-long Eisenhower tunnel, which traverses the Continental Divide. It is essentially the transition from metro-Denver into the mountains of western Colorado. Normally there is a steady stream of traffic going through the tunnel, but on this night it was desolate. There we were, in formation, barreling through the tunnel and running away, as far as we could. And once we got to the other side, I knew my life had permanently changed.

*

We hid out in the mountain home for the entire month of August. I didn't go into the office once. I didn't see patients or conduct any meetings. I did spend much of my time on the phone answering questions for Planned Parenthood and trying to figure out where this was all going to lead. We tried to stay in touch with family and friends as much as possible.

Our nanny at the time was young—only in her twenties—but she was wonderful with the kids. She'd started working with us only a few months before the videos were released. I had told her where I worked right from the start, and thankfully, she was very supportive.

We arranged for her to come out to the mountain home to help us for a few days. She was recently married, so we invited her husband too. We wanted her to be as comfortable as possible amid all the chaos. The mountain home had a separate house on top of the garage, so they both ended up coming and staying with us for a while.

That house in the mountains was beautiful and peaceful. We were very lucky. After a few weeks, the owners had guests coming into town, so we had to clear out. We worked out the timing so that by the day we had to leave the first house, another donor from a different board was able to offer us *their* vacation home for two more weeks. Both of these settings were idyllic places where we would have loved to vacation, but we were never able to truly appreciate our natural environment, even for a moment. We were in such a daze and everything felt so uncertain.

We didn't have the best Internet or mobile phone reception out in the mountains, so I could only believe what I was told at the time: that the "It's a baby" line was all over the news. And then I learned that John Boehner had tweeted about it. Even though it was fake news, it was a huge ordeal.

An Associated Press article from that day read, in part:

The searing political conflict over abortion flared anew Wednesday as three Republican-led congressional committees said they will investigate whether Planned Parenthood is selling organs from aborted fetuses. House Speaker John Boehner, R-Ohio, criticized the group and said President Barack Obama should condemn and end the practice.

The GOP offensive came a day after an anti-abortion group circulated a video it made secretly showing a Planned Parenthood official discussing the disposal of body parts from aborted fetuses.[3]

John Boehner brought a new level of attention to a story that was already making headlines. He said, "When an orga-

---

3   "Congressional Panels Will Probe Planned Parenthood Video," *Chicago Tribune*, July 15, 2015

nization monetizes an unborn child—and with the cavalier attitude portrayed in this horrific video—we must all act."

An oversimplified summary of the abortion conflict is that the anti-abortionists want to extend rights to the pregnancy itself; this has always been part of the battle. So when David dubbed in the "It's a baby" line, they were able to turn around and say, "Look! Even the *doctors* know it's a baby."

Of course, I hadn't said that; it had been dubbed in, but we couldn't prove that yet.

*

We pretty much kept to ourselves during the entire month of August. It was a vulnerable time for us as a family—and for me in particular. Because I had seen how people responded to the videos that came out before mine, I felt that I was going to be judged in the same way.

One time, a colleague said something like, "When I saw the first video, I thought, 'Oh no, I can't believe you said that,' but when I saw the full video, I realized it had been taken out of context."

These people were supposed to be like family, and even *they* were doubting me. My immediate family didn't question me or my integrity, but I knew some extended family members did, and even some friends seemed to have doubts. When I think back on that time, it just felt like everyone was questioning me, doubting me, and judging me.

Planned Parenthood hadn't yet arrived at their *"heavily edited videos"* phrase, which would later be used a lot. It was hard to try to convince people that David's group had dubbed in words when we had no proof of that.

The PR team working with Planned Parenthood hired an outside forensics company to analyze my video, and they had me come in and listen to a particular part of the video with them. At one point, they stopped the tape.

"There's a hum at this part; is that you?"

The experts were able to determine that the pitch was too high. It wasn't a natural sound in the video, and it was clear that the audio had been adjusted. That's how they knew words had been dubbed in. I knew, of course, because those words had never come out of my mouth; they would never even have entered my brain in that situation.

While I was away from the office during the month of August, someone delivered an ominous postcard to PPRM, reading:

Savita, your neighborhood will be visited by Colorado rescuers and your neighbors will receive info about all the videos. If you want to discuss any reasons why the visit would be unnecessary, please contact Colorado Right to Life. We're praying this will lead you to repentance and salvation.

Planned Parenthood security contacted me right away.

"We got this note, and they're obviously going to come to your house," they said.

The good news was that we weren't living in our home. The bad news was that we cared about our neighbors and didn't know what kind of a scene this would cause. Many of our neighbors knew us well, and we had made a good effort from the very beginning to be a real part of our neighborhood. We had lived there for seven years—since 2008. It's so easy for life to feel busy and to use that as an excuse not to get to know who's in your neighborhood. But I knew that, because of my job, it was essential that we get to know people from the beginning.

And so we did. Since the videos had come out, neighbors had been reaching out to me. But once we found out about the postcard, we wanted to try to get ahead of the situation. I sent a long e-mail to the neighbors we knew, explaining what was going on. They were all grateful for the heads-up, and seemed glad to know we were safe. The group of neighbors who we'd e-mailed formed their own little crew and went around to inform the rest of the neighborhood about what was going on: letting them know what to expect, informing them that the police had been contacted, and—most importantly—telling them not to be afraid. They really helped us get the word out to the people we didn't know personally.

That group of neighbors became our boots on the ground. When the anti-choice people later came into the neighborhood and distributed flyers targeting me, those neighbors were the ones who went around, picking them up.

We had security cameras and other means of surveillance, so we could see all the protestors clearly, and were able to document their activities and send the recordings to law enforcement and others as needed.

After that, the anti-choice people took things one step further and mailed individual flyers to every single house in our neighborhood.

*

I was told that the protesters had significantly increased their presence outside Planned Parenthood. They would call on all their followers to come out and protest, and on a few occasions, there were around seven hundred people outside the PPRM administrative building. Before all the videos came out, there used to be maybe ten people protesting on an average weekday, maybe twenty or thirty on a weekend. Sometimes they would throw a big carnival-like party outside of the PPRM building—a protest party.

But after the fake videos came out, there were days when hundreds and hundreds of protestors would show up. Across the country, some Planned Parenthood locations had thousands of protestors. And of course, after my two videos came out, they handed out flyers with my name and photo on them—and made sure to include links to the fake videos.

After a full month away from our home—in two borrowed mountain houses—we knew we had to find a more permanent place to live. My husband had to get back to work, and I wanted to get back to town too. Besides, I couldn't drive three hours in and out to take the babies to their doctor appointments. But after hearing what the FBI said and having more than one suspicious person outside of our home, we just didn't feel that it was safe to go back there. My heart was broken.

We asked Planned Parenthood to help secure a safe living situation for us. They got us into a furnished apartment in Boulder for the first week of September. They definitely went through some hoops to get this arranged for us, and we still had our security guard, paid for by Planned Parenthood. But by this point, I felt like I only wanted security with me when I was going to and from work. We were about to move into a new place, and no one knew we were there. We felt anonymous. But as we prepared to move into the apartment and get our lives back on track, we lost an important piece of the puzzle.

Our nanny had been wonderful to us—especially through such a trying time. But the whole infiltration, the videos, and the ensuing media mania were hard on her, to say the least. She was young, and all of this made her anxious. She knew that Susan Sutherland had taken her photo outside of our house and, understandably, this freaked her and her husband out. The sense of responsibility she felt for the babies only added to her anxiety.

One day she broke down crying and said we needed to talk. I knew that she supported me 100 percent, and that this was the reason why she was so torn up. But at the same time, I couldn't deal with someone who was that emotional. With everything that was going on, I had zero bandwidth to support another person; I was barely keeping myself together. I needed to feel secure about who was looking after my kids during the day. There were constant distractions.

I told her, "I understand how hard this is. You need to take care of yourself and your family first. I will figure this out."

She left that day.

*

When I returned to work, things weren't calmer. They were worse. Soon after, John Boehner said, "We must all act," and called for an investigation of Planned Parenthood. The House Energy and Commerce Committee sent a letter to Cecile Richards, then president of the Planned Parenthood Federation of America and president of the Planned Parenthood Action Fund, requesting my presence in front of this congressional committee in order to answer questions. Similar requests were made of Deborah Nucatola, Mary Gatter, and other providers who had appeared in the videos that had been released. We were being deposed for a special hearing to discuss the nature and content of those videos. My interpretation was that they were trying to make Planned Parenthood admit to practices that were potentially illegal. So, at the end of September 2015, I flew to Washington, D.C., for an entire week.

The week that I was there, I barely ate. I was sick to my stomach the entire time because I was so stressed out. My husband stayed home with the babies, and my parents flew to Colorado to help him take care of them. None of us knew what to expect. *I* was being called to speak to congress? *Me?* Savita Ginde from Ohio? None of it felt real.

I remember my parents and husband saying things like, "Stay strong," "Be honest," "You know how to do this," and "You can handle it." It was all pep-talk sort of stuff. They were trying to be strong for me, but deep down we were all terrified.

We didn't even know if Planned Parenthood was telling us everything. Did I have all the information I needed? Even today, I'm not sure I have ever been told 100 percent of what they knew about the infiltration. Everyone was on a "need to know" basis, I guess. But there I was, picking out clothes to wear for standing in front of congress.

It felt like I was a pawn in somebody else's game. What did I have to do with this whole thing? I wanted to get this horrible episode behind me as quickly as possible—but on the other hand, I was pissed. My entire life had been thrown into a blender.

*

On my flight to D.C. for the meeting, there was a lady sitting next to me who kept looking at me strangely. We had a brief conversation during the early part of the flight, and I knew that she was from the Denver area. As we deplaned, she turned to me and said, "You know, you look really familiar."

This very situation had become a persistent occurrence and concern for me—that people were going to recognize me. I remember saying something to her like, "Maybe we go to the same gym." I just made it up because we were both flying from Denver. She looked perplexed, and I quickly walked off the plane. I was always worried people were going to see me and think, "That's the video lady!"

My time in Washington began with three full days of prep with the legal team. Planned Parenthood had hired a firm that had done some congressional briefings before. They helped us prepare for the type of questions we might be asked, and what our answers should look like based on the truth.

I ended up having the shortest hearing of anyone: under two hours. The Planned Parenthood lawyer thought it was because of how I answered the questions. I did great. I was really on my game. I was honest and clear, and I made it a point to talk specifically about the falsified audio on the video.

It didn't matter to me that all the people present for my briefing somehow believed the fake videos were real. Nevertheless, my lawyer knew it was of utmost importance to me to make certain the committee knew that words were dubbed into my video. So, when the opportunity presented itself, I was able to introduce everyone present to the fact that words were added into the videos—and that I have *never* participated in fetal-tissue research or exchange of any sort.

Everyone present had no choice but to hear what I had to say. It felt like much of the committee was trying to make us admit to something we hadn't done. I took every opportunity to vindicate myself.

While my briefing was short, other people were in there for hours. Cecile Richards' televised hearing was insanely long—like five hours or more. Hers was an official deposition, whereas mine was considered a briefing.

After my briefing concluded, I flew home that same day. My briefing got very little attention in the press because it had taken place on the same day that John Boehner had resigned.

*

I returned home and tried to get back into the swing of things: getting through the morning routine with the babies, going to work, seeing patients, and meeting with colleagues. Eating dinner. Getting through the nightly routine with the babies. Sleeping as much as possible. Repeat. We knew we could stay in the new apartment for at least six months, which gave us a little bit of time to just settle in and breathe. I thought I was going to have some time to regroup. But on some days, my husband had to remind me that I needed to eat or do other basic things. My days were spent struggling to get any amount of sleep, attempting to work, and trying to spend as much time with the kids as possible. I was having a hard time. I often felt like I was in a fog. I was having difficulty remembering things.

I don't know if I was depressed, but I definitely was out of sorts. I'd always been someone who had a plan, but during this time, that was impossible. I didn't feel like I had all the pieces I needed on the whiteboard in my head to create a game plan. I couldn't think straight. It felt like I was in limbo, and I realized I had to let things shake out a little more. I knew, deep in my gut, just as I had when I exited the Eisenhower Tunnel on August 3, 2015, that my life had changed. I was just trying to figure out what my best next step would be, and I knew my thoughts were too jumbled for this to become apparent to me anytime soon.

The protesters outside Planned Parenthood had increased in number over time. Because of this, I would always arrive at the office extremely early so I didn't have to walk past any protestors. I would leave the apartment around six o'clock in the morning and wouldn't head home until late in the day, after the protesters were gone.

Those days were really long. I always asked the security guards to check their monitors before I left the office. I didn't want anybody following us home. I still had private security driving me to and from work, thankfully. I never drove in or out on my own. This helped keep my husband's and my parents' fears at bay.

Later that month, we heard from a few neighbors that our FBI contact and a US Marshal were back in the neighborhood. At this point, we had been out of our house for several months, though my heart still ached to go home.

The neighbors said these law-enforcement folks had been taking pictures all around our house and talking to people throughout our neighborhood. They informed the neighbors that they were just there to take some pictures, but when one particularly freaked-out neighbor asked why, the agent said, "Just in case anything happens." This was unsettling information, to say the least. It seemed like that should be unfathomable.

In regard to the videos, I remember waiting for weeks with bated breath for Planned Parenthood to come out with some type of statement. Something that defended us from the false allegations and fake news. I wanted them to say, "These are our providers, and they do good work. These videos are all lies."

And I probably gave them a little bit of grace at that point, because they were paying for my private security and had helped us secure the apartment. It felt like they were trying to be supportive of our needs. It didn't all come crashing down until a public meeting in November, at which Cecile Richards asked for it . . . and I gave it right to her.

CHAPTER 7

WHAT DOES "FORWARD" EVEN MEAN?

NOVEMBER 2015.

Every year we attended a national conference called the North American Forum on Family Planning. I had attended this conference for the last fourteen years, and I sat on the National Medical Committee because of a board position I had within the medical-director leadership at Planned Parenthood. I was a part of the large group that makes decisions about the policies that govern our patients' daily care across the country.

I had already registered for the conference, which was in Chicago that year, but when the videos came out, I e-mailed the conference organizer to let her know that I was going to cancel my registration. She understood, but told me that she was going to keep everything in place for me just in case I changed my mind. A close friend who lives in Chicago reached out and said that she was going to attend, and that she wanted to see me, even if just for a couple of days. She said we could room together, and I began to think that maybe it was a good opportunity to reconnect with some colleagues and be in a safe space after all that had happened.

Looking back, I realize I was naïve. I had a Pollyannaish vision of what it would be like when everyone was there. I thought Cecile Richards would get us all together and we would be able to let our hair down and have a real conversation about what had happened. But I should have known that an organization as politically involved as Planned Parenthood would never let that happen. They would never let their hair down with us, I would never know the entire truth of how Daleiden was able to infiltrate the organization without being recognized. It's kind of sad, because I feel like it was owed to us. I feel like we deserved some measure of transparency and respect—which Planned Parenthood denied us by failing to create the conditions for the candid conversation we needed to have.

In a general sense, it was good to see my colleagues, although it was also a little surreal. A lot of people asked me questions about what happened, which was fine; it gave me an opportunity to get the truth out there. I got a lot of support at the conference because everyone there knew that the videos were fake. When the fake videos had launched earlier that summer, I'd begun to receive an outpouring of calls, e-mails, and letters of support from within the family planning community and from many personal friends. This was now the first time I was seeing many of these same friends and colleagues in person.

At the same time, I didn't really have all the answers yet. I didn't know where I was going or how to move forward. I was in a state of limbo. There were so many questions on my mind: *How am I supposed to move forward? When am I allowed to move forward? What is it that gets me there? And what does "forward" even mean?*

One morning was particularly strange. They did this session for which they put together a compilation of all the edited videos and brought in a trauma expert to talk to people. It was supposed to be some sort of a processing exercise. I was asked by Planned Parenthood if it was OK to show portions of the video in which I was portrayed, in some type of learning tool. I told them they could use whatever they needed to if it was being used in a constructive manner. However, I also told them that I was not going to attend that session and that I was not going to watch it or any related video. Absolutely not. I had never fully watched any of my videos and I had no intention of ever doing so. I didn't need to see any of that stuff, not even a snippet, ever again; it is all fake. But they didn't seem to fully understand where I was coming from. They sent me the link for whatever compilation they created from all the fake videos, but I never clicked on it. I am still not interested in anything related to Daleiden's fiction.

Later that day, there was the annual luncheon at which Cecile Richards usually gave a great, emotional speech and got everyone all riled up and ready to fight the good fight. This time she was very emotional.

She seemed nearly in tears when she said, "I threw my prepared speech away. I think we should have a very open discussion." They had done the video trauma-resolution processing exercise that morning, and I heard that some people had made some very emotional comments (for all the right reasons). Things had come up that needed to be resolved. This was really the first time the Planned Parenthood community had all been together in one place since the videos had been released.

There were about four hundred plus people in the luncheon ballroom, and instead of giving her big speech, Cecile took the opportunity to open up the room and give others a chance to talk. They passed out microphones, and I grabbed one.

I told her everything. I said, "I don't know if this would have prevented things, but my husband e-mailed you in 2011 about our serious concerns over safety at Planned Parenthood. Instead of responding, you punted that e-mail to my CEO, Vicki. And Vicki—oddly enough in a women's-empowerment organization—sent me an e-mail and told me to 'manage my husband.'"

I pointed out that her own chief medical officer had asked *me* for security help on the very day my video came out—while my life was unraveling. I told her that despite what was happening to me and my family, I had sent her chief medical officer my PowerPoint safety presentation.

Now the one thing I did not mention prior was that early on in this video scandal, the Planned Parenthood national office held a video conference call with all the medical directors from across the country, providing security tips and information. As I sat on this call, I was flabbergasted to see that the safety and security presentation they were walking everyone through was foundationally the one I had sent to their chief medical officer just a week or so before. Sure, they had added and updated a few things, but it was clear that they'd plagiarized the work my husband and I had done, and didn't bother to give us credit or appreciation.

I called her on it. The national office had presented our hard work to the medical directors from across the country as if it were work they had been doing on security for years.

I told her that this was wrong. I was emotional. I was angry that we had lost our house and our freedom. I was angry that we couldn't live at home anymore because it wasn't safe. I was angry that Planned Parenthood had basically washed their hands of all that and declared that the loss of safety in our home wasn't their problem. I was angry that they'd put us in this position. I was angry because I felt like my husband and I had done everything we could to prevent exactly *this* from happening. We had fought tooth and nail to try to improve security at work for years—but, I told her, "You blew us off every single time."

The room was silent. Cecile didn't respond. I think she was taken aback. I didn't realize how emotional I had become until after I had put down the mic. There was so much going on and I wasn't going to miss the opportunity for my voice to be heard. Everything just spilled out.

When I sat down, a friend turned to me and whispered, "I think she heard you."

I looked down at the white place settings on the table and felt my hands shaking. Adrenaline was still pumping through me. I remember the CEO from the Michigan Planned Parenthood, Lori Lamerand, looking at me, eyes wide and apparently seething. I knew she would run and report this to Vicki. She clearly didn't have an ounce of empathy.

In that moment, I remembered Cecile calling me, months before, on the day my second video was released. She had called to say she was sorry. I didn't really know what to say at the time; I think I just said thank you. But I remember thinking, "Thank you for the support—but what are you going to do about all this? What is the organization going to do?"

*

A couple of days after I returned from the conference, I received an e-mail from Vicki, stating that we really needed to meet. This was when she really began to show how self-absorbed and narcissistic she really was; this is when she really became, in my eyes, wicked.

I went to see her, and once I walked into her office, I didn't leave for hours. She said that everything was entirely my fault. She told me how terrible I was, and how David Daleiden and his people had only gotten in there because I had brought them in. She leaned in hard on me—I'm guessing because of what I'd said to Cecile. It felt like payback. She said I hadn't represented the organization well when I'd made those comments publicly to Cecile. I sat in silence for most of the meeting.

What she didn't understand was that it wasn't about Cecile. The sad part is that, for the most part, Vicki and I had been on pretty good terms before all this; we had worked together for nearly twelve years. As she turned on me and berated me, the phrase *This can't be happening* kept repeating in my head.

When the videos first came out, I thought that everyone was being so supportive. But I realize now that we were all like deer caught in headlights. Everyone was so caught off guard that all we could do was cling together to get through it. But because I was accustomed to dealing with high-pressure situations, part of me knew that at some point it was all going to fall apart. Because it always does. Once people have time to process a disaster like this, it's natural to start pointing fingers. I think that's a common human reaction to any crisis. But allowing Vicki (who never took the security of PPRM seriously enough) to blame me for the colossal shit show that was David Daleiden and his fake company, Biomax? I wouldn't have that.

She hadn't even been at the conference where I had spoken publicly to Cecile. Everything she'd learned about it was hearsay from colleagues. She said she'd heard that it was "a big yell fest." I told her it wasn't, and politely reminded her that people were emotional at the conference because these events had affected many people's lives—not just mine.

I admit that the open-mic moment at the luncheon was intense. But I think it needed to be, and I needed to say what I did. I have no regrets.

Sometimes people are uncomfortable with candor, but I believe that sometimes you have to be willing to push the envelope and to ask the tough questions to get to the point where everyone can say, "OK, now everything is on the table. Let's figure out what we're going to do."

I realized then that Vicki was not only wicked, she was too disconnected from everything that had happened. She was shielded from it. She lived in a bubble. These were just words and stories to her; she didn't understand what it was like to be attacked on social media, by e-mail, or in phone calls, and actually to feel like her life was in danger. She didn't know what it was like to run away from your house, babies and diapers in hand. Or to have round-the-clock security because the FBI and your employer feared for your safety. Anytime something similar happens to her, she uses it to leverage sympathy and donations—money that pours in but is never used to improve the security for Planned Parenthood's staff or providers.

I told her all of this, and I added that she didn't have good pulse reading of what was going on. But it is what I said next that haunts me—not because I regret saying it, but because instinctually, I was so right.

"You do not understand the level of venom and violence that exists out there," I said. "Mark my words, the next thing that's going to happen is someone is going to get hurt." I said to Vicki that the intensity of emotion over these fake videos was so high that I worried about violence escalating—and that it seemed inevitable that someone was going to get hurt. She looked at me like I was crazy, and as usual, she blew me off. She made it clear that she was completely out of touch.

I pushed back: "I don't think you get it. People are questioning the ethics and integrity of Planned Parenthood right now. It's not just that they don't like *me*. People don't like *Planned Parenthood* right now—and for you to think that the staff and their families are safe is crazy."

Four days later, a man named Robert Dear, who had seen the fake videos online, went into the Colorado Springs Planned Parenthood with a gun and killed three people.

*

I got the worst text of my life on a Friday at around eleven o'clock in the morning. It was the day after Thanksgiving, November 27, 2015, and many of our Planned Parenthood locations were slow and operating with half the normal staff because of the holiday. I wasn't working that day, so I was at home with my family. My stepson was in town, and I remember it being a lazy morning. We were still lounging around and trying to enjoy a rare relaxing family day of quality time with the babies.

That's when I received a text from one of my physicians, Dr. J.T. Boyd, who was working in our Colorado Springs location that day. At first, I briefly thought he might have been playing some kind of a bad joke but soon enough the reality became clear and the seven words on the screen were the fulfillment of my very worst fear:

There's an active shooter in the building.

I felt paralyzed, and the hairs on the back of my neck stood up straight. I shouted for my husband and he immediately contacted the FBI and turned on his police scanner to try to confirm what was happening.

Colorado Springs is over two hours away from Boulder, so we were nowhere close to the event. We turned on the news and my stepson Googled "active shooter Planned Parenthood," but nothing was up yet. Dr. Boyd said someone had already called 911, and that he and four other people were hunkered down in a physician's office. His phone battery was low and he didn't want to lose the ability to reach someone, so what seemed like long periods of time would pass without us hearing back from him. It was terrifying. He told me he'd put his phone on silent to prevent the shooter from hearing it if it rang.

I texted my boss and told her that I was in touch with Dr. Boyd, and I knew that FBI, SWAT, and local police were on the situation. The next step on our end was trying to determine who was working that day and which families we needed to reach immediately.

By this point, the story was breaking all over the news.

After an incredibly long five-hour standoff and various law-enforcement tactics and strategies to minimize further harm to innocent people, SWAT teams crashed armored vehicles into the lobby and Robert Dear surrendered. Fortunately, my colleague and all our staff had made it out alive. Three other people, however, had been killed: one police officer and two civilians. The police officer, Garrett Swasey, was off duty at the time, but he had bravely and heroically responded to reports of an active shooter. The second victim, Ke'Arre M. Stewart, was only twenty-nine years old, and according to reports, he had tried to run into the clinic to warn others before being shot himself. The third victim, Jennifer Markovsky, had been accompanying a friend to the clinic.

Robert Dear had also shot nine other people—four civilians and five police officers—with multiple semiautomatic rifles; these people survived. Court documents state that Dear believed his actions "saved lives of other unborn fetuses." When he was captured outside the clinic, he issued a chilling callback to a phrase we had all become far too familiar with by that time: "They kill babies in there. They sell baby parts."

That sickens me to my core. The "baby parts" phrase comes from the videos. This shooting was directly linked to the illegal actions of David Daleiden and Center for Medical Progress. This shooting and Robert Dear's actions were the direct result of fake news.

In a 2016 *Atlantic* story, journalist Matt Vasilogambros wrote, "Dear also shot at propane tanks in the parking lot, hoping they would explode. Before the standoff with police even began, Dear approached a woman outside the clinic and told her, 'You shouldn't have come here today,' before shooting her multiple times in the arm."[4]

*

It was a horrible day. The tragedy cut into me deeply. Part of me felt like if I hadn't been in those videos—if the infiltration had never happened—maybe this crazy guy wouldn't have killed those people. At the time, this was one of *my* health centers. I'd worked closely, regularly, with many of the staff; I considered many of them like family.

Court documents would later reveal that Dear had a history of gluing the locks outside of other clinics to prevent patients from seeking care. Dear also idolized Paul Hill, the man who had killed an abortion provider and his bodyguard in Florida in 1994. He believed President Obama was the antichrist.

The Colorado Springs clinic staff was traumatized, obviously. Dear had walked up and down the halls for an extended period of time, shooting randomly. The survivors said that while the crisis was in progress, they continually heard gunshots but didn't know who was possibly being killed. They had friends and patients in the building, and

---

4   4 Matt Vasilogambros, "What the Planned Parenthood Shooter Wanted," *The Atlantic*, April 12, 2016, https://www.theatlantic.com/national/archive/2016/04/planned-parenthood-shooter/477825/

they sat there, hiding, hearing what sounded like people getting murdered right outside the door, and thinking that they were next. I can hardly imagine what that was like; I am even horrified to recount it now.

Our clinics were meant to be open the following day—Saturday—and one of the biggest decisions I have ever had to make in my life was whether or not to close down that Saturday and negatively impact our patients, given the events that had just occurred.

I was working at one of the health centers and my partner physician was meant to work at another. When I called him, I said, "We need to make this decision together. Either you and I are both working, or we are not."

We had been assured that there would be increased armed security at our health centers. I said that we could ask for whatever we felt we needed if we were going to stay open—or we could contact all staff and say we were standing down. Everyone would take the day off.

We decided that we were going to stay open. It was the scariest day I've ever had at work, but I had to do it. We felt that we had to stand strong and not give in to terrorism.

The analytical part of my brain thought *The probability of that kind of violence happening again in another Colorado Planned Parenthood on the very next day is pretty low.* Then the other part of my brain fired back, *Yeah? Or is it a series of attacks and we're going to have them at all of our other sites?* Somehow I found a way to manage this anxiety. I just rolled up my sleeves, traveled to work with my armed security, and looked my staff members in the eyes.

"We're going to do this, together," I said. I wanted to be real with my colleagues. Not just because I was chief medical officer, but also because I was a provider, just like they were. "Let's just be real with each other. I know we are all scared to be here."

I tried to build a plan for the day as logically as I could.

I said, "Let's think about *right now*. If someone dangerous comes in, what are we going to do?"

All of us made a game plan that day on how to defend ourselves. We figured out which doors we would run through and how we would get our patients out.

When our patients showed up, they were astonishingly grateful that we were there. They were thankful for the work we were doing, especially under the circumstances. Some patients had been at the Colorado Springs location the day before but hadn't been able to get their procedures taken care of before the shooting began, so they'd had to come to us the following day. Wow. These women were determined to have their needs met. Their resilience was empowering. I imagine the fear they were feeling was similar to ours. Throughout the day, patients told us, "Thank you for doing this," and "Thank you for being here."

As we fell into a basic rhythm that day, I thought of all the people who had struggled for decades to make a woman's freedom to choose a legal right. I considered the men and women who had fought for this right. I thought of the citizens who had lost their lives the day before in Colorado

Springs. But more than anything, throughout that day, I said to myself, "David Daleiden, look at all that your fake videos have done. None of this is good. You should not be proud of your deceit. All of this bears on your soul, and any feeling of triumph on your part is hollow."

CHAPTER 8

PROTEST THE CAUSE, NOT THE PEOPLE

WE ARE AT war with ourselves.

On most days when I see patients, I arrive early, take care of administrative tasks, attend meetings, catch up on e-mail, and then change into scrubs to head into the clinic. Every now and then a nurse from the clinic will call, page me, or even run up to my office, depending on the need.

On several occasions, the purpose of the call has been to notify me that one of the patients has been recognized as a protestor who has previously demonstrated outside our very clinic. The first time this happened, it took me a few minutes to digest what I was hearing. The hypocrisy is astonishing: Yesterday this patient was out there yelling, bullying, and harassing other women for coming into the clinic—and today, she's here to have her abortion!

I have performed abortions on women who have stood outside my building and terrorized me, my staff, and my patients. Bottom line: We know that people on both sides of this issue use the freedom that Roe v. Wade grants them.

And it isn't just me. I have spoken with colleagues, and I know that many providers across the country have treated protestors as patients. I have had patients tell me directly that they have protested outside. I remember one patient saying, "I am not like any of the other sluts and whores that are in here getting abortions."

Another said, "I cannot believe I am getting this done. I promise that tomorrow, I will be right back out there protesting."

It's hard to know how to respond to a statement like that. I tell them that I don't understand. It really puts a provider in a tough spot, because we are there to take care of the patient and not to be judgmental—regardless of where she stands on the issue of abortion.

So I typically say, "I don't completely understand where you are coming from, but it is up to you to decide how you want to behave."

These are adults, and they can make their own decisions, but I wish they would think a little more deeply about the harm they cause other people around them and how disingenuous they are being with themselves.

These situations require a real gut check. I do my work and treat some of those protesters as patients because I believe deeply that once a woman is fully informed and educated about accurate resources and options, the decision is for her to make in consultation with whomever she finds appropriate. Nothing else she says in that room matters to me. When a woman comes to me as a patient, I support her right to make decisions about her body, despite the terrible things she may have said or done outside our clinic. I have seen the signs they hold up with my name and picture on them, with the words "Baby Killer" next to my face. And now one of those people is here, in a gown, in my office, telling me that she needs an abortion because of an unplanned pregnancy. Believe me, it is tough.

*

There is no bridge between the two opposing sides. Anti-choice. Pro-choice. It feels like everyone has taken his or her stance and now clings to it with every ounce of energy at their disposal.

Let me be clear: Would it be so bad to reduce the number of abortions in America? No, it wouldn't. But I want to do it the right way, and I will fight every day for a woman's right to choose what is best for her and her family. Putting laws in place that say you cannot have an abortion, or that you cannot have an abortion without jumping through impossible hoops, is surely not the way to reduce the number of abortions. Those who can afford to have their needs met always find a way. Laws simply make women who are already struggling just struggle further. These laws make women feel marginalized—or, more likely, further disenfranchised—and this only creates further division.

Did you know that the word *abortion* is not even found

in the Bible? The scripture passages often cited by conservatives have nothing to do with abortion. To their credit, Evangelicals and the Religious Right concede this point, but they claim that teachings about abortion are implicit in scripture. This, of course, is entirely dependent on one's interpretation of the Bible, and herein lies the problem.

Writer Michael J. Gorman articulates this conflict perfectly in his paper "The Use and Abuse of the Bible in the Abortion Debate":

> Some years ago I overheard an argument between two women, one "pro-life" and the other "pro-choice," about what the Bible has to say on the subject of abortion. The pro-life woman appealed to Deuteronomy 30:19 in support of her contention that the Bible opposes abortion: "I have set before you life and death, blessing and curse; therefore choose *life* . . . ." The pro-choice woman responded quickly, appealing to the same verse in support of her belief that the Bible promotes freedom of choice: "That's right," she said. "'*Choose* life.' There has to be *choice*."[5]

As the religious right ramped up their fight against abortion, an interesting hypocrisy emerged: there is nothing about their behavior that aligns with their religion's message.

---

5   University Faculty for Life, http://www.uffl.org/vol%205/gorman5.pdf

We are told that religion is about kindness, love, forgiveness, and helping other people. But I don't see any of that in the actions of these religious protestors. I see no kindness or love outside our clinic. There is not even a pretense of helping other people when protesters try to block women from receiving legal treatment.

The truth is, the Bible can be interpreted in many different ways. You can always find a verse or a passage that will say what you want it to say. You can interpret the language and the lessons however you want in order to make your point. In some ways, that is probably the beauty of the book, but that fluidity is used to fuel violence, intimidation, and bullying.

People who engage in this type of Bible bending—the ones who say it is OK to harass and threaten violence against a person because he or she is an abortion provider—need to think twice about this. I ask them to pause and really think about what they're doing. I don't think those actions reflect their religion; they are dishonorable and unacceptable behaviors in a civilized society. Maybe they should ask themselves, "What would Jesus do?" I am pretty certain that this is not how Jesus would have behaved.

Contrary to what many people may think, it is possible to have a solid, religious or spiritual foundation *and* be prochoice. I am—I have been a part of Colorado's Religious Coalition for Reproductive Choice (CORCRC) since 2013, and I am currently on their board of directors.

*

It's OK for us to disagree about abortion. I believe in our freedom as Americans to think and feel differently from one another. We do not have to agree that there is only one answer here. But we should agree that our basic rights to freedom and peace should outweigh all other concerns.

I hope that those who are against abortion will always have access to the information they need to make informed decisions about their lives. I do not try to convince those who are against abortion to suddenly support it. What I care about is that every individual in this country has the right to make up his or her own mind. Why can't we let our fellow citizens choose for themselves?

My mantra for a long time has been, "Protest the cause, not the people." Maybe it's time we developed some rules of engagement here. Our freedom of speech and our right to protest are the cornerstones of our society. Those freedoms are indispensable—but they shouldn't infringe on another person's right to a peaceful life.

Protest the cause, not the people. Do not come to my house. Do not take photos of my children. Do not slander me online and threaten me on Twitter. Do not harass my family. I believe it is 100 percent acceptable for American citizens to peacefully protest outside a Planned Parenthood facility. That is their right. But the purpose of coming to a healthcare provider's home is to intimidate him or her, to scare that person and his or her family, and possibly to turn the neighborhood against that person. The idea is to establish ill will between our families and our communities. We have a basic human right to be able to live peacefully in our homes. We must raise the bar here in terms of the basic humanity with which we treat one another.

The protesters came to my neighborhood with grotesque signs, forcing my neighbors to have uncomfortable conversations with their kids. Some of those signs bore photos of what looked like a seven-month-old baby, beneath which were written slogans accusing us of killing babies. No one wants to see that, and it's an inaccurate description of what we do. It's intended to incite anger—which it definitely does. But it's also an infringement on my privacy and security. I don't know what kind of religion would promote this kind of behavior.

Their actions did accomplish one thing: 90 percent of our neighbors ended up thinking of the anti-choice people as domestic terrorists and hated them.

One neighbor wrote to me soon after we fled from our home, in response to the e-mail I'd sent out attempting to explain why we were leaving and what they might experience in the coming weeks. This neighbor does not believe in abortion, but I was touched by the manner in which she articulated her feelings about what was happening to my family:

I appreciate your e-mail and I will just say that I am most definitely pro life and have never been a fan of planned parent hood because of this and other reasons. That being said I am sorry the harassment that has been happening to you and your family. Picket the facility but don't harass people in this aggressive, angry way. I am sure everyone of us in this neighborhood and in this world have been a part of something that is not what God would be proud of. Christ asked the mob, when the women caught in adultery was brought to him, any one among them with out sin to cast the first stone. None did and walked away but what happened after was even more telling, he tried to teach her about her sin without threats, demoralizing and scare tactics but with Love. I'm very sorry for what is going on and I will say the same to any of the extremists that ask!!!! Thank you for your e-mail!!! Good luck to you and your family.

She does not support abortion—but she supported me. She understood that the actions of the protesters were inexcusable. The question is: Do we want to help one another become better and more constructive citizens of a shared society—or do we want to perpetuate a zero-sum culture war that leads to division, violence, and murder?

According to the FBI, domestic terrorism is perpetrated by individuals and/or groups inspired by or associated with primarily US-based movements that espouse extremist political, religious, social, racial, or environmental ideologies. The US Code of Federal Regulations defines terrorism as "the

unlawful use of force and violence against persons or property
to intimidate or coerce a government, the civilian popula-
tion, or any segment thereof, in furtherance of political or
social objectives." (28 C.F.R. Section 0.85).

I believe that the protesters who made my life a living
hell are terrorists, plain and simple. When they came into our
neighborhood and distributed hateful material about me,
they were trying not only to terrorize me and my family—
but also my neighborhood. They frightened everyone who
drove down our street. They terrorized my neighbors, who
explicitly told them, "We do not want you here."

They attempted to bully and intimidate my family, but
they also had a larger impact on the entire town. Their threats
stretched the resources of our police, who had to make sure
no one was getting hurt in our neighborhood. The protesters
trespassed on our property, requiring the police to take action
when they otherwise could have been attending to the other
needs of the town.

Fortunately, their terror tactics backfired, arousing the
anger of our neighbors, who came out to support us instead
of shunning us. Those neighbors didn't necessarily come out
in support of me because of what I do for a living; they stood
by us because they don't believe in bullying and intimidation tactics, and because they were appalled by the protestors'
methods.

We have spoken to many people across the country
who have also been harassed by these terrorists and they all
said the same thing: 90 percent of their neighbors supported

them and found the protestors truly disgusting and horrible.

Many anti-choice people say that these extremists are just that—extremists—and that they don't represent the beliefs of the majority of their movement. But I would ask them to look at it differently. If you're an anti-abortion activist, you need to recognize that this behavior is essentially the core of your movement. If you don't put a stop to this kind of bullying, intimidation, and violence, you are all responsible.

David Daleiden is responsible for the threats to my safety and for the tumult my family endured, and in my opinion he's responsible for the deaths of three people in Colorado Springs. He is responsible, as are all the other vocal and activated anti-choice people here in Colorado and everywhere across this country who stand with those who incite violence. They need to be held accountable.

We need to take a hard look at the intolerance that exists in our society. When people push their religious views on you, they are sending you the message that your belief system isn't as "right" as theirs is. Remember the postcard that was sent to me at work? It said, "We're praying this will lead you to repentance and salvation."

But I don't subscribe to your religion, so why are you applying your rules to me? I think we have to take a serious look at this as a culture and as a country. Because as far as I remember, my United States government and social studies classes taught us that this country was built on the concept of religious freedom. Do we really want to make America great again? Then let's start talking. Let's stop the division.

*

If the moral standards of the anti-choice movement are imposed on other people and abortions are made illegal, women will be forced to see their pregnancy through to childbirth. Do you really want to force someone to give birth who is saying, "I am not able to have a child," "I am not ready to have a child," or "I do not want this child"? What kind of a society would that be?

And the hypocrisy doesn't end there. Look at how these right-wing, anti-abortion groups want to cut programs that have been established to help women who have babies they can't financially support. None of it makes sense. If you believe it's OK to force a pregnancy on someone, then shouldn't you also believe that that person should have access to resources to help the child? No woman should ever be put in this position—period. But if we are going to restrict abortion access, don't we need to offer resources to help the mother from that child's birth up until the age of eighteen? Anyone who has ever had a child knows it is not easy.

*

This "war against women" extends beyond the discussion about abortion. Women are more a part of the workforce today than ever before, and they are taking on greater responsibilities, far beyond the scope of their original roles as wives and mothers. Many women are career-oriented and feel that they can't have kids; they are working all the time, trying to get ahead. They don't feel that they have the time and attention to maintain the forward momentum of their careers *and* build successful families.

And then there are millions of women, like me, who are trying to do both. It is a struggle because the appropriate resources are not allocated to women in this country. The fact that some women don't get time off for maternity leave is considered ridiculous in most countries, particularly in Europe. Many women have to use their allotted sick days not for the times when they are sick, but as ad hoc maternity leave.

We have not done enough as a country to support the transition of women into these greater roles outside the home. For me, and for so many others, it feels like I have two jobs: I am a mother *and* I am a physician. Yes, my husband helps and supports me, but when the babies are sick, even he will say they want their mom. Like many working mothers, I manage my children's schedules and appointments, the nanny, and countless other daily necessities.

Generations ago, mothers stayed home and took care of the house and the kids while the fathers worked. Even I grew up with a working father and a stay-at-home mother. But today, many families cannot support themselves this way. In most working-class and low-income homes, *both* parents need to work.

But as a country we have not evolved to a place where we can support that. Studies have shown that women make more money than their male partners in over half of US families—and yet, they are not offered the support they need from a cultural and societal standpoint. Maternity leave is often inadequate. Hell, we aren't even being paid equally. Women aren't receiving the same opportunities to advance their careers. They are promoted less often and given fewer leadership opportunities than their male colleagues.

I believe that part of this struggle—this war on women—is a result of fear. People are afraid of losing "the way things always were"—the "known" that so many of us grew up with. Change is hard, but if history has taught us anything, it's that change is often necessary.

*

I grew up attending a Catholic high school, which is odd because we were raised Hindu. But I was a curious teenager. I remember once standing in line for Communion because I wanted to see what it was all about. When the wafer was put in my mouth, instead of just accepting it and walking away, I had questions. I took the wafer out of my mouth, held it in my hand, and looked at it. I wanted to see what it was. I have always had this sense of curiosity within me. I laugh now when remembering the incident, but I actually got in trouble for it at the time.

My religious schooling came full circle for me after the fake videos were released. It was a horrible time, and I felt trapped. The headlines kept getting worse and worse, and the attacks on social media were frightening. Sometimes I would get a strong impulse to just run. I wanted to flee. I didn't want to leave my family, of course, but I wanted all the horrible things that were happening to go away.

One day, I ended up at a church in Boulder. I just felt that I needed to be somewhere safe. The church was supposed to be closed, but one of the pastors saw me and opened the door. I just sat there on the stairs, and she sat with me. It didn't matter to me that it wasn't my family's religion. God is God. My belief is that we all see Him or Her in different ways. That is what religion is. I can find solace in another religion's church—and I can still feel the grace of God. It might not be the God that I pray to, but I can still find peace.

For a long time, we didn't have a Hindu temple in the small Ohio town in which I grew up. Eventually, the Indian community built a temple in Youngstown, but until then, our temple was around an hour and a half away, so the Hindu community would rent out the banquet hall of a bank every Sunday, and we would go there and create a community. The Hindu religion doesn't require that you have one place of worship; it is more about the way you behave on a daily basis.

So, the Hindus in Youngstown created this place where we could all come together and pray with our small community. I think community is a big part of what comes out of religion. Every Sunday that banquet hall became our temple.

My husband and I hope to instill in our children a relationship with spirituality and a deep sense of morality. I want them to experience my Hindu culture as best as I know it, and I also want them to learn what my parents have to teach them.

My husband grew up Southern Baptist, but he let go of his religion. He feels there is a deep-seated hypocrisy in the faith in which he was raised, and he abhors the feelings of guilt and disappointment that he believes religion causes. He left his church because he did not agree with the notion that if you don't behave in a pious way, you are doomed to hell. And if you do anything wrong, such as create fake videos that turn people's lives upside down, lead to the murder of three people, and scar many others for life—all you have to do is go confess. How do we promote tolerance when so many people are taught to believe this?

Since the release of the videos, and amid the chaos and danger that followed, I have tried to learn more about the issues at hand. To that end, I sought out the guidance of some religious leaders in my town who define themselves as pro-choice. I wanted to understand how they can maintain this apparent dichotomy in their lives: being both religious and pro-choice.

Many of them talked to me about the freedom of the individual to make his or her own decisions, and the idea that if you are making a decision between you and your God, or between you and your family, then it is *your* decision. No one else should have a role in it except for those you invite to do so.

Judaism teaches that the soul doesn't enter the body until

the first breath. The crux of the fight over abortion is this very question: When does the soul enter the body? When does this growing thing become a *human being*?

This whole notion of life beginning at conception is a fabricated, unprovable position to take. When is it a baby? When is it a life? These are questions that will simply never be answered. We cannot pinpoint the exact time of conception. We know when implantation occurs—but that happens over the course of days.

Repeating something that cannot be proven doesn't make it true. We're at war over an unanswerable question—a war that may continue until the end of time.

Things become even more complex as we look toward the future, and at the role technology plays in medicine. Traditionally, pregnancies used to be considered viable between twenty-four and twenty-six weeks; if you delivered before that point, it was a coin toss whether or not that baby was going to be able to survive. But today, we have twenty-one-week and other very early pregnancies that can survive. Is this not a wonderful thing?

I recently read an article on the website of the National Catholic Bioethics Center. The author, Father Tad Pacholczyk, writes about IVF and gestational carriers, arguing that the mere existence of these technologies doesn't necessarily mean they should be used.[6] "Surrogacy raises grave moral

6   [6] Father Tad Pacholczyk, "The Multiple Moral Problems of Surrogacy, October 2016, https://www.ncbcenter.org/files/6914/7880/1338/MSOB136_The_Multiple_Moral_Problems_of_Surrogacy.pdf

concerns," Father Pacholczyk says, "and powerfully undermines the dignity of human procreation . . . ." I find this argument extremely specious, and seeing a religious leader take this stance is sad to me. It's an attempt to instill a feeling of guilt in anyone who is trying to have a baby with medical assistance. The message is basically this: if you cannot get pregnant naturally, you're just not meant to have a baby at all; you should not have access to any of the technology that is available to help you, because that is not the way things were meant to be. This makes people feel like failures. Who wants to subscribe to *that* religion?

If you don't want technology to be employed to facilitate a pregnancy for someone who wants it and can't get pregnant on her own, then are you also saying that the same technological advances shouldn't be used to resuscitate a pregnancy that is born too early? How do you pick and choose? Again, this all comes down to personal judgment and what you believe—but these questions are going to grow bigger and deeper as medicine advances.

Religious and government leaders stand at pulpits and support agendas—defund Planned Parenthood or make abortion illegal—and these agendas are useful for rallying their troops, but not helpful in terms of finding solutions to our problems. I think we all agree that we want to lower the abortion rate. And if you want to work toward that for religious reasons, fine. But it's not OK to impose your religion on everybody else. If we take religion out of the equation, then I think we might be able to come to the table and talk.

We need to have an actual conversation without fighting, and without threats or violence.

What is keeping us from having this conversation? Why can't we just roll up our sleeves, get the right people together, and map out some solutions that work for everyone? Instead, the anti-abortion movement proposes "solutions" that are really just hurdles for certain women.

It's an attack on the very foundation of this country to say, "Everyone should believe what I believe." That is not freedom; there is only one religion in that scenario. And if we let our policies and laws become intertwined with that religion—well, then we have a theocracy.

The *Merriam-Webster Dictionary* defines theocracy as "political rule by priests or clergy as representatives of God." Is this really the kind of government under which we want to exist? If you're going to be insular and intolerant, or if you're going to suggest that your religion is the only one that counts, then you have more in common with ISIS than you do with your fellow Americans.

We need an exit strategy. We need a map that will lead us away from this road because we are headed for destruction. We need to make these conversations broader and look at what's good for overall public health—not necessarily what's good for people from one religious background or another.

CHAPTER 9

"FATHER, FORGIVE THEM, FOR THEY KNOW NOT WHAT THEY DO"

CAN WE TALK chicken for a moment? Recently, I read an article in the *New Yorker* about Chick-fil-A's expansion into New York City, and about the Christian values that are the very foundation of the company.[7] Many journalists reacted to this article with bewilderment; to them, this was an affront to Christian values.[8]

Do I believe there is a problem with stating specific religious values as a foundation of your business? No, not really. I don't really understand why anyone would want or need to do this, but to each his own. However, I've had some unpleasant encounters with businesses and people who *do*

---

7   Dan Piepenbring, "Chick-fil-A's Creepy Infiltration of New York City," *The New Yorker*, April 13, 2018

8   Kate Taylor, "People Are Slamming a Writer for Calling Chick-fil-A 'Creepy' and Criticizing Its 'Pervasive Christian Traditionalism,'" *Business Insider*, April 13, 2018, http://www.businessinsider.com/people-slam-article-chick-fil-a-creepy-christian-2018-4

claim to represent a specific religion's values, and I question the true motive for a business to make this claim. More often than not, when I have interacted with any person who prides himself or herself on espousing Christian principles, my experience has been a negative one. I have been judged and dismissed.

Just a few months after my twins were born, I twisted my ankle. This wasn't the first time I'd done this; however, it was terrible timing. Anyway, I implemented the basic supportive measures right away, but several days later I was still unable to bear weight on my ankle. I figured it was time to get an x-ray. I went to my insurance website, found an in-network orthopedic practice close to my home, and was able to schedule an appointment for that same day. I felt lucky that I didn't have to go to an urgent care facility. On the way there, with my husband driving me, I Googled the practice to get the office address. As I was on the website, I began perusing their website, when I noticed that the practice was "guided by Christian principles." I read it out loud to my husband, and I said, "I am interested to see what this is all about; maybe that's why they worked us in so quickly."

So we got to the office and my husband helped me hop inside. I checked in and was called back to see the doctor in a matter of minutes. *Very efficient practice,* I thought. A pleasant physician entered the room and we talked about my ankle. He agreed that I needed an x-ray. Then he made note that I was a fellow physician, and the usual chitchat ensued: What type of practice do I have? Where was my practice?

Where do I work?

I answered as I always do: "I provide family-planning healthcare services. My main office is in Denver. I work at Planned Parenthood." And that last statement abruptly ended our conversation. He stopped talking. He stopped making eye contact with my husband and me. He handed me a sheet of paper, pointed me in some direction, and said, "Your x-ray is there." He then turned around and walked out the door. I looked at my husband and said, "OK, well, what started out as a great experience just went down like a lead balloon." I had said the two words that tend to allow some individuals to exhibit poor-quality, disrespectful, dismissive behavior: "Planned Parenthood."

After I got my x-ray, the doctor returned to the room, again with no eye contact. By this point, I had apparently become a burden to his day. He threw the x-ray up on the light box, said, "You are good, everything is fine," and then turned around and walked out.

Are these the Christian principles that guide this practice? I'd describe it as rude, condescending, and unprofessional behavior. I am not interested in these types of "guiding principles." How could anyone be?

Many months later, I was relaying this story to a friend. I am still astonished by the experience that I had with this orthopedic practice, which, at the time, was located in Louisville, Colorado, but, to my surprise, now appears to have expanded. The funny thing is, my friend told me that her husband had a similar experience at the same practice. She's the one who taught me that the phrase "cornerstone" can imply Christian principles. Again, I am not sure exactly which Christian principles are guiding the practice, but I am not interested in experiencing this type of behavior again. I don't see how Jesus would have ever promoted such behavior. I must have missed that day during my religion class in high school.

On a different occasion, over ten years ago, I was in Colorado Springs with some friends and colleagues. We went to a local eatery during happy hour, and there happened to be a group of men there from a local Christian church. A couple of the guys came over to my friends and me and started talking. Questions similar to those I was asked at the orthopedic practice arose: What's your name? Are you from the Springs? What do you do? Where do you work?

We each answered appropriately. When we got to the "Where do you work?" question, a couple of us replied, "Planned Parenthood."

In response, these men literally just turned around and walked away. Didn't say another word. Did not excuse themselves or find some respectful way to decline further conversation. It was just rude and inappropriate. I'm not sure what sort of principles their church had instilled in them, but that kind of behavior is not OK.

I know that I am not the only one having these untoward experiences. These behaviors—coupled with the behaviors of those anti-choice protestors who descended on our home, harassing and trying to intimidate me, my family, and my neighbors—don't turn me off to Christianity as much as they turn me off to people's belief that they have to state their religious affiliation. What's the point of saying, "I am a Christian"? I'd rather experience what I believe is the true foundation of Christianity, and, for that matter, most religions. I want to experience the love, kindness, respect, and compassion that lies at the very core of many religions. Don't *tell* me; show me.

Does claiming to be Christian or to espouse any other religion's values as the guiding principles for a business, or even as the foundation of one's sense of self, give one the right to judge, mistreat, and fuel negativity, and thus, division? Those who *live* their religion are probably less likely to feel the need to *announce* their religion.

Even in my current job, the one I started after I departed PPRM, I have had eye-opening experiences—twice. During my interview, I was appropriately transparent about all this fake news and my experience over the past few years. After I had already accepted the position, my then boss called to tell me that I had been Googled. Because of what had popped up in a Google search of my name—mainly the fake-news articles and links from Mr. Daleiden's fantasy adventure—questions had been raised, and concerns voiced by devoutly Christian executives and staff members who were concerned about my joining the team. I was being judged even before anyone knew who I was or what my guiding principles were. No one had even experienced the caliber of the skill and abilities that I could deliver. I wasn't due to start my job for another two months, and yet I already had critics because of the propaganda Mr. Daleiden and his supporters had sold to the world as fact in order to push their personal agenda and portray anyone who wasn't going to join their fictional bandwagon as someone who was a less-than-perfect Christian.

I offered to speak directly to anyone at my potential new workplace who had questions or concerns. I was ready to stand tall and clear up this gross misunderstanding when, to my amazement, I heard the following words come out of the mouth of my Christian boss: "I want you to know that I have taken care of these concerns and you do not need to do anything. I did want you to be informed though. If anything like this comes up again, I will, without question, always stand by you."

Wow. I had not heard that level of clear, unfettered support and solidarity from anyone outside of my family over the past two years. It still makes my heart swell with emotion to think about it. I felt a strong connection and dedication to the truth with someone who held beliefs different from my own; it was amazing.

So I started my new job in July 2017, and hit the ground running. Within two months, it was Groundhog Day, so to speak. A new physician executive, a devout Christian, was joining our team. I was Googled, and he judged me. I'd never even met this new physician, but, he had significant concerns about me and wanted to make sure the CEO, executives, and senior leadership were all aware of who I am, what I believe in, and the fake news that was displayed in my Google search results. In return, I judged him back: small-minded Christian who believed that his way was the only right way, and who had fallen prey to Daleiden's propaganda, poor guy.

Once he started his job, we were advised by our boss to meet. I embraced the opportunity to model the fact that people who hold seemingly different *guiding principles* can actually work together. His personal beliefs and my personal beliefs have no place within our healthcare delivery system or in our workplace. Our concern, our duty, is to meet the needs of our patients, provide them with resources that support their beliefs and meet their needs, regardless of whether those beliefs are in line with or different from our own.

Remember those protestors who have come to Planned Parenthood for an abortion? Despite the schism in their souls, we still provided them with the same high-quality experience we deliver to all our patients. No judgement was ever verbalized to them by the Planned Parenthood staff. I would then presume that one would strive to apply a religion's guiding principles uniformly—or are they meant to imply that if your beliefs are different, then you should not expect to be treated the same?

It really boils down to one question: What's the point of publicly defining oneself as a Christian or as a follower of any other religion? I don't think it should matter. People either behave with love, kindness, respect, and compassion, or they don't. When I was growing up, I never knew people's religions; now, it seems everyone has to announce it. Then, many take the values of their religion and apply them to you, whether or not you subscribe to or understand them.

Colorado Right to Life asked me to seek repentance and seek salvation. I really don't know what that means. Why are we trying to push our individual beliefs on others? I know several people who are personally against abortion, but who tell me that they would *never* force those views on anyone else. Shouldn't people make their own decisions about something this important? And how much sorrow must envelop the anti-choice protestor who seeks out an abortion but has no voice and no support?

We can all disagree about the way we want to live our lives. We can even disagree about what we think is right or wrong. But each free person in this country should be able to live without threats, harassment, and intimidation based on differing beliefs.

When I grew up in the 1980s, there was a ubiquitous billboard ad for United Colors of Benetton. It featured all different shades of people on it—different races, characteristics, and backgrounds. It's not like we haven't been a more tolerant society in the past. But for whatever reason, we have become less tolerant over the past twenty or thirty years. Today, it seems that we define ourselves more by what separates us than by what connects us.

Nowadays, if a boy wears makeup, there's the potential for uproar in his school or community. Transgender kids are threatened every day. Compare this climate to the atmosphere of the 1980s: Prince and Michael Jackson were two of the biggest pop stars. Duran Duran was a sensation. Those boys wore makeup, but no one cared. If someone looked like that now, however, he would likely be cyberbullied out of school. Why *is* that?

How can we get back to a place where we are proud to be a true melting pot? I wish that instead of fearing what is different, we could be curious about it. Having an interest in someone who is different from us, or being curious about a different religion and wanting to learn—that's what makes us people. We are different, and yet we are the same. Curiosity and knowledge-seeking should be the values we aim to teach our kids—rather than dismissiveness and judgment.

As much as I realize the importance of being cautious and aware of the dangers that are ever present, I believe that we should not use the necessity of caution as a license to discriminate, or to think that if someone is different from us, it means they don't belong here. I think that since 9/11 we have lost a little bit of our curiosity about people who are different from us. The guardrails went up, and I think they are too high.

We have lost a little bit of our humanity too. Fear and suspicion of people who are different from us doesn't make us safer. It only puts us at greater risk of hurting one another.

*

If we truly want to help reduce the number of unplanned pregnancies in our society, let's do it realistically. We need to find a way to separate our individual religious beliefs from this discussion. We are losing sight of the true goal.

If the goal is to help people become constructive, productive contributing members of a diverse and tolerant American society, and, as a part of that goal, reduce the number of unplanned pregnancies, then let's put religion aside and actually sit down and talk about what we need to do to accomplish that goal. Based on my experience in this field, I have two very simple suggestions: unrestricted access to birth control and age-appropriate sex education.

Passing laws that limit women's access to care will not lower the number of abortions in America. This will only discriminate against those who are already struggling.

Anti-choice laws are not the solution. Let's start with the facts: People have sex. People have sex when they want to have children. People also have sex with no intention of having children. Sex can be an important part of a healthy, balanced lifestyle.

Kids need valid, balanced, fact-based sex education—and birth control should be easily accessible. The goal should be to reduce the number of unplanned pregnancies so that people can have life structure, so that they can focus on the parts of their lives that are important to them, be that school, or work, or the kids they already have.

This also means that people need access to *reliable* birth control, as well as the education that will enable them to select the methods that work best for them. Instead of basing teen sex education on an abstinence approach, we should be realistic. Teens are going to be curious about sex. Abstinence-only education has been proven ineffective,[9] so let's get our heads out of the sand. We need to develop age-appropriate education for teens so that they understand the normalcy of hormones, why deciding to become sexually active should be a well-thought-out decision, how to use birth control, and how to be safe. This will drive down the number of unplanned pregnancies in America.

Sexuality is part of a healthy lifestyle; we have to stop being embarrassed about this. Only if we are realistic about that can we achieve our shared goal of reducing unwanted pregnancies. The best thing we can do is get people age-appropriate education so that they can make the best decisions for themselves.

*

In this country right now, there is a law that allows for the termination of a pregnancy. Period. If you don't believe in abortion, don't have one. We need to use more accurate language if we want to achieve our goal. The statement should not be, "Stop killing babies." It should be, "Let's reduce the number of abortions." And the best way to do that is to provide birth control and education for people who are going to have sex.

---

9   Kathrin F. Sanger-Hall and David W. Hall, "Abstinence-Only Education and Teen Pregnancy Rates: Why We Need Comprehensive Sex Education in the U.S.," National Center for Biotechnology Information, U.S. National Library of Medicine, October 2011, https://www.ncbi.nlm.nih.gov/pmc/articles/PMC3194801/.

*

Access to accurate information has never been more under threat. President Trump didn't coin the term "fake news," but he made good use of the phrase, and now it feels like we can't get away from it. Fake news turned my life upside down. The entire video campaign that David Daleiden and the Center for Medical Progress created is based on lies. The facts were fabricated. The videos that included me were edited to manipulate context, with words and phrases that I never said dubbed in and attributed to me. I've never done fetal-tissue research, so for them to come out and say that I was selling baby parts is the very epitome of fake news. A quick Google search perfectly illustrates this problem.

Here are some top headlines from 2015, from reputable sources, dissecting the edited videos and the infiltration:

- "Planned Parenthood Deserves to Be Supported, Not Attacked" (The *Washington Post*, July 16, 2015)

- "What the Planned Parenthood Hoax Really Proves: Right-Wing Extremists Have No Qualms about Destroying Peoples' Lives" (*Salon*, July 16, 2015)

- "Undercover Video Sting of Planned Parenthood Is Off-Base, as Usual" (The *Los Angeles Times*, July 16, 2015)

- "Abortion Is a Medical Procedure. The Reality of Those Often Isn't Pleasant" (*The Guardian*, July 15, 2015)

- "That Planned Parenthood Video Isn't the Scandal Abortion Opponents Are Making It Out to Be" (*Cosmopolitan*, July 14, 2015)

- And yet, when you search my name online, these are among the top Google results:

- "Planned Parenthood VP Says Fetuses May Come Out Intact" (Center for Medical Progress)

- "Planned Parenthood Sought $1.5 Million from George Soros After Exposed Selling Baby Parts" (LifeNews.com)

Our access to information is skewed. Most people are going to Google something and then quickly scan the first page of results. Few people ever click over to a second page, let alone dig through multiple pages just trying to find a respected news source covering a story like this. It's scary that this is the way the majority of the world gets its information.

*

Everybody deserves access to valid information so that they can make decisions about what is right for them. And that means that the anti-choice people are going to have to digest the fact that some people are not going to do exactly what they want. And that's what this country is about: people having access to information and then being able to decide what is best for them. Otherwise, are we truly a democracy?

For better—and for worse—the Internet connects everything and everyone. Everyone has access to his or her own microphone. We have become a "sharing culture." Information spreads much more quickly than it used to, and can unite people on either side of any given coin. It can also make people feel like they have to join or support a cause simply *because everyone else is doing so* and no one wants to be left out. It enables people to connect with one another . . . and it allows religious terrorists to organize and influence as well.

The internet connects people, but it also makes those connections more *visible* to the world at large. This makes it easier to rally folks around a cause, especially when using propaganda. And perhaps people have become more engaged in causes because we are able to connect so easily, transcending space and time in a way that we never could before. But there is also a snowball effect: people are becoming bolder in their positions and more emotional in their reactions to the world.

People feel more justified in their extreme reactions to things because they can always find an information vacuum— an online community of people who agree with everything they think and feel. Unfortunately, this can open the door to mobilize that lone wolf with a cache of guns—someone like Robert Dear, who watched those videos, believed them to be true, and went on a rampage.

*

My video was a complete joke. David Daleiden manipulated the audio and added words to make it look like I did something that I have actually never done and said things I actually never said. Congress spent millions of dollars calling us to D.C., forming a committee, and conducting a baseless investigation. They didn't find a damn thing. After over a year of investigations, the Congressional Select Investigative Panel dissolved and has not reformed. Democratic congresswoman Jan Schakowsky released a statement about the matter:

> History will not look kindly upon this Panel. Panel Republicans spent nearly $1.6 million taxpayer dollars chasing inflammatory lies being peddled by anti-abortion extremists. Their inappropriate working relationship with these groups put law-abiding doctors and researchers at risk.
>
> After fifteen months investigating the secretly-recorded and deceptively-edited video allegations, Panel Republicans have uncovered no evidence of wrongdoing. Yet, rather than "follow the facts where they lead," as Chair Blackburn promised, Panel Republicans ignored them.
>
> They have repeatedly made false claims, including a series of "criminal referrals" to federal, state, and local law enforcement officials based on unsourced, unverified documents and infor-

mation. In some instances, Panel Republicans recycled claims of anti-abortion extremists that [had] already been investigated and dismissed.

The Panel's so-called "final report" is illegitimate. Under the resolution, the Panel—not just its chair or majority members—must issue the report. Republicans refused to give Democratic members the opportunity to review the report, failed to hold the required public meeting, and ignored the requirement that the full Panel vote on its release.

This Select Investigative Panel leaves behind a legacy of lies, intimidation, and procedural misconduct. It will be remembered, like the House Un-American Activities Committee and McCarthy hearings, for its excesses and abuses of power.

CHAPTER 10

#BEBEST

CAN WE EMBRACE the First Lady's #BeBest campaign as something we can model for the children it is intended to help? I hope this book encourages self-reflection and open, respectful conversation. I hope people across our great country will come to the table to talk about these issues— about freedom, safety, health, acceptance, and education.

We must find a path that will help us rise above all the division and negative rhetoric. We should try to find some lessons in this nightmare—some way to alter the conversation we're having about abortion and equity and justice for *all* women. I dread the possibility that all this could end up having been for naught, and I would hate for this ever to happen to *anybody* else.

My boys are growing up and getting big. Many years from now, I will tell them about this time in our family history. But how? How will I explain a story like this? How will I teach them about basic human rights, the importance of equity, and about things as complicated as religion, abortion, and freedom?

How will I teach them about resilience and tolerance,

and about fighting for what they believe in, and the importance of equity, and for caring for more than just themselves? If anything, I think my story holds many examples of how people should *not* behave—too many such examples, if you ask me. I will tell them that what these people did to us is something they should never do to anybody else. If I accomplish nothing else by writing this book, I hope to shift the conversation to a more positive direction. If there's anything I can do in the wake of this nightmare, it is to stand up and boldly speak the truth as a good example for my children.

I want people to have a better understanding of the impact of their actions—of what unfounded, ill-intended, propaganda-based harassment can do to a family. We can't let this happen in our country. We are better than this, and we should *be better than this* to one another.

The phrase "Make America great again" has been imprinted in all our minds, for better or for worse, since the 2016 election. I say let's do it—but let's do it the right way. Let's be respectful of one another. Let's protect the freedoms for which people came to this country. Let's raise the bar on how we behave. A difference of opinion or belief is never an excuse for violence. It's not a reason to bully, harass, or intimidate.

I don't have all the solutions, but I know we can't go on this way. As citizens of this country, we should be asking for something better.

#BeBest

AFTERWORD

(Written by my husband)

THESE PAST FEW years have been an eye-opening experience. I still can't believe this happened to us. The negative impact of extremism and fake news is significant. It is all around us and affects all of us in one way or another. Just turn on the TV, browse YouTube, or read through the comments sections under blogs, online news outlets, social media, and other areas of the Internet. It is easy to see that as a nation, we are more divided than ever.

The David Daleiden videos were utter falsehoods, and yet, nearly every news station and even many of our esteemed congressional leaders believed them. I think it would behoove us all to think more critically whenever we consume media. It seems that *everything* is now being politicized and taken out of context in order to create or perpetuate misleading or downright false narratives. Unchecked confirmation bias and incivility seem to be the rule rather than the exception.

This, and the prevalence of extremism, will further divide this nation and continue to lead to violence. This, in turn, will challenge our ability to maintain unity, and even law and order.

When I first walked into the Colorado Springs Planned Parenthood building on that December day back in 2015, just days after the shooting, I was horrified by the extent of the carnage. A familiar location where I had walked my wife into work many times—where I knew many of the caring staff members and the manager like they were members of my family—was literally riddled with bullet holes in every direction. I remember the wave of nausea I experienced as I pictured what it must have been like to have been in that building with an active shooter. Over the years I have personally engaged in hundreds of law-enforcement and tactical self-defense training scenarios, including active-shooter and home invasion exercises. All this training has made me a stronger individual, but none of it fully prepared me for the emotional impact of the real-life aftermath of all this. It hit too close to home.

I was angry that David Daleiden had created that fake story in some sick effort to advance his extreme ideology, and apparently for his own fame. I was angry that this story involved my wife, who has never done fetal-tissue research. She does not sell, nor has she ever sold, fetal tissue.

Nonetheless, she and I do support research into life-saving and life-altering treatments and cures. Like many people, we have friends and family who could benefit from the treatments and cures that this research promises.

As someone whose mother lost a happy and rewarding nursing career to retinitis pigmentosa (for which there is still no cure) in her mid-thirties, I would have paid anything to have reduced her suffering and improved her life. From the time I was a young boy, I watched her struggle through the cruel progressive loss of her vision. As the world she knew changed, so did mine. It was tough on her, and it was tough on our family. Luckily, she is a fighter and a strong woman, fiercely independent to this very day. She somehow managed to raise four boys even while steadily losing her sight. She was over 90 percent blind before I was even in middle school. Why would anyone stand in the way of improving someone else's life? That little boy asks this very question to anyone who would force his or her ideology on others—and today, this man asks that same question.

If your beliefs require you to take a stance against stem-cell research, then please, don't partake in any of the life-saving and life-improving benefits that might arise from such research. Don't get vaccinated. Don't accept any of the cures for horrible diseases—like polio or blood cancers—that have resulted from stem-cell research. But *please* don't stand in front of that young boy and tell him that his mother can't get treatment or can't get better because researchers are prevented from using stem cells by your own personal religious beliefs. That's bullshit.

Will you deny the world a cure for the dementia that eventually killed my grandmother? Or a cure for the diabetes that killed my father at sixty-five, before he could really start enjoying retirement? Will you deny us a treatment or cure for the cancer that ravaged and killed my own brother at the age of fifty-one?

Maybe you would. Maybe it doesn't matter until it is *your* mother, *your* father, *your* brother. I think we should do better for and demand more of one another.

I have always believed that if you must lie to make your point, then you don't really have a point. Having been raised Southern Baptist, the Jesus that I know would *never* support or promote the malevolent lies of David Daleiden and those like him.

Daleiden and his cohorts had no regard for the potential ramifications of their actions. I was truly saddened by the level of media attention lavished on these videos, and saddened that so many people (including some of my own family members!) could believe them. And even after the fake videos were debunked, many in the media continued to report on them as if they were newsworthy.

In seems that news is only labeled fake when it hurts one's own cause. At least more people have begun to closely scrutinize the media they consume. Hundreds of people have contacted us to tell us they were sorry that they had been fooled by those videos (although, incredibly, the videos are still circulated and continue to be believed in certain circles to this day).

The whole hysteria generated by the videos culminated in the Colorado Springs shooting—in the murder of law-enforcement officer Garrett Swasey (a forty-four-year-old father of two young children and an elder in his church) and other innocent people, the wounding of several other police officers, and the scarring of many for life. This did not have to happen. David Daleiden bears the weight of all this devastation on his soul. He will have to answer for all of it. It was his malice that caused this catastrophe.

The journey that this family has been on for the past couple of years has been at times exhausting, but it has made us stronger. The journey has been both enlightening and disappointing. We've had hurtful experiences. We've seen the true colors of people we once called friends—and even family. We have eliminated these people from our lives, and though our world has become a little smaller, we have benefitted by removing the negative, unsupportive, and ill-intentioned. Most of all, we have felt love and support from many people whom we only knew from a distance at the time that all this occurred.

We are truly indebted to those who lent us a helping hand, regardless of the fact that we were complete strangers —as Jesus would have done. These humbling moments have restored our faith in humanity, and we consider ourselves blessed.

Our boys are resilient. They are strong, and yet also kind and loving. As toddlers, they ask a *ton* of questions, and we encourage them never to shy away from asking tough questions to get to the truth. My wife and I are doing our best to encourage their critical thinking so they can do their part to make the world a better place. Our hope is that they will fight the good fight—because humanity's needs and the greater good supersede anyone's narrow individual beliefs, however strong.

CPSIA information can be obtained
at www.ICGtesting.com
Printed in the USA
FFHW01n1728181018
48843407-53044FF